Engaging with Faith
Family Devotional

ENGAGING WITH FAITH FAMILY DEVOTIONAL

70 Fun Activities for Christian Families to Strengthen Faith

JENIFER METZGER

ROCKRIDGE
PRESS

First Rockridge Press trade paperback edition 2022

Rockridge Press and the Rockridge Press logo are trademarks or registered trademarks of Callisto Media Inc. and/or its affiliates in the United States and other countries and may not be used without written permission.

For general information on our other products and services, please contact our Customer Care Department within the United States at (866) 744-2665, or outside the United States at (510) 253-0500.

Paperback ISBN: 978-1-68539-143-0 | E-book ISBN: 978-1-68539-213-0

Manufactured in the United States of America

All Scripture quotations are taken from the Holy Bible, New International Version®, NIV®. Copyright © 1973, 1978, 1984, 2011 by Biblica Inc.® Used by permission. All rights reserved worldwide. All other quoted material is in the public domain.

Interior and Cover Designer: Carlos Esparza
Art Producer: Hannah Dickerson
Editor: Brian Skulnik
Production Editor: Ruth Sakata Corley
Production Manager: Riley Hoffman

All illustrations used under license from Shutterstock.com

10 9 8 7 6 5 4 3 2 1 0

To my husband
Jeremy, I love you always & forever.

To my children and grandbabies
You are all my blessings from heaven, I love you.

To my parents
Thank you for giving me a strong foundation.
I love you.

CONTENTS

INTRODUCTION

Welcome to *Engaging with Faith*! I am so glad you are here. I feel honored to be a part of your family for the next seventy days!

My husband and I have four children, plus two daughters-in-love, and one son-in-love, whom I call "My blessings from heaven." We also have two additional blessings: a grandson and a grandbaby on the way. Grammie life is the best life!

In addition to being a mom of four, I homeschooled our children, and I worked in children's ministry for nearly three decades, eighteen of those years as a children's pastor. Raising and teaching children has been my life!

I've always had a passion for teaching children about Jesus. There is something so precious and so beautiful about watching the lightbulb come on for children when they learn about Jesus and begin to understand His love. Through my work in children's ministry, I have seen children cry with joy when touched by Jesus, pray powerful prayers for one another, and begin their own journey of faith. I've also seen parents come to Jesus through the faith of their children.

My prayer is that your family will learn to spend quality time together around the Word of God and this book will give you the tools you need to help your children learn about Jesus and understand His love. I also pray that you, as parents, grow in your relationship with God throughout this journey. And finally, I pray that lifelong memories are made as you establish a family devotional time together.

The next seventy days are going to be wonderful! Are you ready for this?

Sweet blessings,
Jenifer

HOW TO USE THIS DEVOTIONAL

This devotional consists of seventy devotions, designed to enjoy as a family. Although it may sound ideal to go through the devotions in seventy consecutive days, that isn't always possible, due to juggling schedules and daily adventures. Use this devotional at your own pace. For your family, it may be easiest to do one devotion each time you sit together for dinner, or at breakfast before school, or maybe you commit to dedicating one night a week, giving yourself over a year of devotions! Any way you do it is the right way.

Each day you will find a Bible verse, a short devotion, a reflection to recap the day's devotion, an activity, and a closing prayer. The activities are meant to be off-page and done as a family. Some days your activity will be all about fun, and other days your activity will be more about digging deeper with the biblical theme of the day. I encourage you as parents/guardians to read the activities in advance so that you can gather any supplies needed for that day and be prepared for the conversations that the devotion will generate.

All Bible verses are from the New International Version (NIV), unless otherwise stated. However, I also love the Christian Standard Bible (CSB), the New Living Translation (NLT), the New King James Version (NKJV), and the English Standard Version (ESV). Feel free to refer to your favorite version.

Have patience with one another as you work together to meaningfully engage with the Bible, God, and each other, and apply the lessons to your lives. The key is to learn, grow, and have fun!

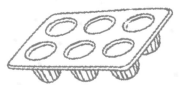

70 DAYS OF DEVOTIONS

IN THE BEGINNING . . .

In the beginning God created the heavens and the earth.

—GENESIS 1:1

The Bible starts out with some powerful words. Before anything else existed—before ice cream, before TV, before social media, before sports, before anything ever was—there was God, and He created everything.

God created the heavens and earth, the night and day, the sky and sea, produce to eat, the animals, and even us. God is a master artist, and everywhere we look we see His artistry skills. We see His handiwork when we look at the puffy clouds, mighty trees, beautiful flowers, shimmering lakes, animals, and so much more. It is as though God had a giant paintbrush and went to work creating our big, wonderful world. And He did it all for you and me. He created it for us to enjoy and take care of.

When someone creates something for us because they love us, we should be thankful and cherish or take care of their gift. It is important for us to appreciate and take care of the world God created and gave to us.

LET'S REFLECT!

1. Think of the very best gift you've ever received. Share what that was.

2. Have you ever thought of the world as a gift from God?

LET'S DO!

God gave us a present when He created this big, beautiful world for us. Today, we are going to spend time enjoying this gift. Are you ready? Go on a thirty-minute nature walk. Try the local park, a nearby hiking trail, or just find some nearby trees. But for the first fifteen minutes, walk in silence. No talking and no phones. Just look closely at God's creation and listen carefully to what you hear. For the next fifteen minutes, talk to each other about the things you like most about God's creation and why. Give each person a chance to share without interruption. Once everyone has a turn, pray, and give thanks to God for His big and wonderful world.

Father, thank You for the world You created for us. Everything You made is good. Help us to appreciate Your gift and take care of everything You made. Amen.

HE CREATED US

So God created mankind in His own image, in the image of
God He created them; male and female He created them.

—GENESIS 1:27

God is a master craftsman; we can see that just by looking outside our window! Genesis continues by telling us that God also created people. He created you and He created your family. God is the Master Artist who created an amazing masterpiece: you.

Each person in your family is special, a special part of God. He created you on purpose. You are not an accident; He didn't mess up or make a mistake. The Bible tells us that He knit you together in your mother's womb (Psalm 139:13).

He created you for a purpose. God has a plan for your life. When He created you, He made a plan that is just for you, and it is good (Jeremiah 29:11). You might not know exactly what every step of the plan is yet, but you will continue to learn as you grow.

Each person in your family is special and created by God. We are part of His beautiful painting, all different, yet all coming together in a masterpiece.

LET'S REFLECT!

1. When you paint or color a picture, do you use only one color or many different colors? Why?

2. Our differences are from God, and they make us beautiful and unique. Do you think this world would be interesting or boring if we all looked the same?

LET'S DO!

Today, we are going to get crafty! Gather paper and crayons, markers, or paints. If the weather is nice, you could use sidewalk chalk on your sidewalk. Have everyone draw or paint a picture of themselves. Take your time and be as detailed as you can. On your paper next to your drawing, write out Genesis 1:27—parents or older siblings may need to help younger ones. Once everyone is done, show your drawings to each other. Compliment each other's drawings, and mention one thing about it that you find inspiring. Afterwards, put the drawings together as a family picture. Let this be a reminder that just as you used your artistry to create your drawing, God used His artistry to create you.

Father, thank You for creating my family and me. Help us remember that You created us on purpose and for a purpose. Help us remember that we belong to You. Amen.

TRUSTING EVEN WHEN IT MAKES NO SENSE

Noah did everything just as God commanded him.

—GENESIS 6:22

After the creation story in Genesis, people began to spread out all over the earth. But over time, they began to do things that made God sad. So God decided He needed to start over. But there was one man who pleased God: Noah. God wanted to save Noah and his family, so He told Noah to build an ark to hold his family and pairs of animals because He was going to send rain to flood the earth.

Here is the thing, before God sent the rains, it had never rained before. Ever! No one knew what rain was. Noah could have told God, "There is no such thing as rain! I am not doing the work to build a big boat!" Rain didn't make any sense because they had never seen it. But Noah obeyed God anyway.

Even though it sounded impossible, Noah did everything God told him to do. He built the ark, assembled his family along with two of every animal, and he waited for the rain to come. If he hadn't trusted the guidance of God, they all would have died. It is important to listen to and trust God even when it doesn't make sense. It is also important to listen to our parents, even if it might not make sense at the time.

LET'S REFLECT!

1. Has there ever been a time you were told to do something, but it didn't make any sense to you?

2. Do you find it easy or hard to trust God when things don't make sense. Why?

LET'S DO!

Noah built an ark like God told him to do. An ark is a giant boat. Today, let's build a giant ark-like fort! Using blankets and pillows, build your fort. Then, get your pets, stuffed animals, and family and go inside the ark fort just like Noah and his family did. While you sit inside your ark fort, talk about the story of Noah's ark and how we can trust God enough to obey Him. Make sure everyone gets a chance to share without interruption. End your time in the ark fort with prayer. Then, make sure everyone lends a hand to clean up the mess!

Father, we thank You for the story of Noah's ark. Thank You for teaching Noah to trust Your guidance even when it didn't make sense. Help me to trust and follow You, even when I don't understand. Amen.

JOY FOR TRIALS

Consider it pure joy, my brothers and sisters, whenever you face trials of many kinds, because you know that the testing of your faith produces perseverance.

—JAMES 1:2–3

Reread today's Scripture verse. Did you catch it? The Bible tells us to consider facing difficulties as pure joy. Can you imagine? When things go wrong, when life is hard, the Bible wants us to be joyful!

Why should we be joyful with trials? The Bible tells us to find joy in the trials because when we face hardship, when we face struggles, we can grow our faith in God. When things go bad, we learn to lean on God more than on our own strength or the world. Leaning on God helps our faith to grow, and that is always something to be joyful for!

But *how* do we find joy in our trials? Should we get excited because we are sick or jump for joy when we fight with our friend? No, of course not. What we can do is go to God. We can take our trial to Him and ask Him for help. We can ask Him to show us how we can grow in the trial. And we can lean on Him for strength.

LET'S REFLECT!

1. Think of a recent hard time you had. Were you happy with the trial?

2. How do you think it would have been different if you had taken it to God and trusted Him?

LET'S DO!

The Bible tells us to consider it pure joy when we face struggles. That sounds wild to our minds, but we now know why and how we can find joy during the trial. Today, let's do something fun that will bring lots of joy and laughter. We are going to put on a comedy show! It's important to remember that God gave us joy and laughter to balance out the difficult times. Each of you should come up with three to five family-friendly jokes to share. Pop some popcorn, grab some sodas, and get a flashlight to use as a spotlight, and make a stage space. Let each person have a chance to be in the spotlight and share some funny jokes. Remember, it can be difficult to get up on stage. So, no booing, only encouragement, and lots of laughter!

Father, thank You for the reminder to go to You in our trials. Help us remember that when we seek You in the middle of a struggle, we can be joyful because our faith is growing. Amen.

FORGIVING WHEN IT IS HARD

Bear with each other and forgive one another if any of you has a grievance against someone. Forgive as the Lord forgave you.

—COLOSSIANS 3:13

The Bible tells us the story of Joseph and his brothers. Joseph's brothers were jealous of him, so they made a plan to get rid of him! The brothers threw him into a pit and then later sold him to the Egyptians as an enslaved person. But they told their father wild animals had eaten him.

God protected Joseph and he didn't stay enslaved for long! Instead, he became second-in-command to the Pharaoh. Then one day Joseph's brothers came to the palace where Joseph lived, but they didn't recognize him at first. The brothers did wrong to Joseph. Because of them, Joseph lost his parents, his home, his family, and for a little while was enslaved. Joseph could have been angry and thrown them in prison or even worse. Instead, Joseph did something so amazing—he forgave them.

Sometimes forgiving someone is hard. When they do wrong to us, we don't want to forgive, we want to get even. But God tells us to forgive others. God forgives us when we do wrong, and He wants us to forgive others, just as He forgives us.

LET'S REFLECT!

1. Share a time that someone did something wrong to you.

2. Did you find it easy or hard to forgive them?

LET'S DO!

When we hold on to all the wrong things people do to us, it is like blowing up a balloon. Every time someone does wrong, it is like we are blowing a big breath into the balloon. The balloon will continue to grow until suddenly, it pops. If we hold onto anger, one day we too will pop from the pressure. It is not good for us. Give each person a balloon. Practice blowing up the balloon and seeing how big you can get it before it pops! Alternatively, get a water balloon and see how much water it can hold. When you are done, talk together about forgiveness. If anyone needs to forgive someone, pray together as they forgive.

Father, thank You for forgiving me when I do wrong. Forgiving others isn't always easy. Help me to forgive when someone does wrong to me. Amen.

SPECIAL FOR EVERY DAY

Keep this Book of the Law always on your lips; meditate on it day and night, so that you may be careful to do everything written in it. Then you will be prosperous and successful.

—JOSHUA 1:8

Cake is delicious, isn't it? Chocolate, strawberry, carrot, red velvet—oh my! There are so many yummy options to choose from! But how often do you eat cake? Do you eat it every single day? Probably not! Cake is typically for special occasions. We have it on birthdays, anniversaries, and holidays. Cake is something special we eat when we are celebrating something big.

The Bible might be something special, but it is much different from cake. The Bible isn't only for special occasions. In fact, the Bible is for every single day. In the book of Joshua, we are told to keep the Bible always on our lips and to think about it day and night.

The Bible is from God. He inspired about forty different people to write the words of the Bible. That means that God breathed His words into these people for them to write down. The Bible is like a sweet letter from a friend and an instruction manual all in one. It helps us to know who God is and what His heart is. We need to make the Bible a part of our everyday life so that we can get to know God and live a better life.

LET'S REFLECT!

1. How often do you read your Bible as a family?
2. What are some of your favorite family Bible stories?

LET'S DO!

The Bible is special but not only for special occasions. Today, we are going to do something that involves the Bible and cake! As a family, whip up a batch of cupcakes. Let everyone have a hand in making the yummy treat. While the cupcakes are baking, gather your Bibles, some pens or markers, and some paper. Have everyone choose one Scripture verse and write it on a piece of paper. When your cupcakes are done, put a Scripture verse and a cupcake together and deliver them to a neighbor or relative. Be sure to save a few cupcakes for home too!

Father, thank You for the Bible. Thank You for the special gift that is for us. Help us remember to make the Bible a part of our life every single day, not just on special occasions or at church. Amen.

LOYALTY LIES IN FAMILY

But Ruth replied, "Don't urge me to leave you or to turn back from you. Where you go I will go, and where you stay I will stay. Your people will be my people and your God my God."

—RUTH 1:16

In the Bible we read about a woman named Naomi, who was married and had two married sons. Sadly, Naomi's husband and sons died. Naomi told her daughters-in-law to go back to the towns they came from. One girl left, going back to her hometown. But the other girl, Ruth, didn't want to leave. She wanted to stay with Naomi.

Ruth loved Naomi and was loyal to her. She promised to stay with her always and care for her no matter what happened. Ruth traveled with Naomi when she returned to her own hometown; here, Ruth took care of her mother-in-law.

Ruth taught us to be loyal to our family. But what does loyalty really mean? To be loyal means to be faithful and committed. When we are committed, if we make a promise, we try really hard to keep it. We are there for our family and help take care of them. Family is special, a gift from God. We live in a world where everyone looks out for themselves, but we need to be sure that we are always loyal to our family.

LET'S REFLECT!

1. Do you think it was hard for Ruth to be loyal to Naomi? Why or why not?

2. Discuss what loyalty to your family looks like.

LET'S DO!

Today, we are going to make a movie. As a family, write a short story about someone who is loyal to their family. Come up with a character, a setting, and a premise. Then, set up a camera or smartphone and act out the story. You can record your movie as many times as you want so that each person gets a chance to play your lead character. Be sure to use examples of loyalty from your discussion. When you are done, get the whole family ready for a movie night—jammies and popcorn included—and watch your movie.

Father, thank You for the lesson from Ruth and Naomi. Help us remember to be loyal to You and each other. Amen.

NOT TOO SMALL FOR GOD

David said to the Philistine, "You come against me with sword and spear and javelin, but I come against you in the name of the Lord Almighty, the God of the armies of Israel, whom you have defied."

—1 SAMUEL 17:45

Do you ever feel like you're too small or weak for something? We all do at some point. In the Bible, David teaches us that with God, we are never too small.

Goliath was a giant. He was over seven feet tall! Not only was he tall, but he was also strong and mighty. David, however, was just a small child. Goliath was ready for battle with his war armor and sword. David was too small to wear war armor and too weak to carry a sword like Goliath.

When we look at David and Goliath, we think there is no way David could stand up against Goliath and win. But David understood something very important, he knew that God was with him, and he was not too small for God to use him.

It doesn't matter how young or small you may be, and it doesn't matter if you feel weak or insignificant. God can always use you. He has a special plan for you and needs you to be willing to do His work.

LET'S REFLECT!

1. Have you ever felt like you were too small or too weak for something God wanted you to do?

2. Do you think the lesson from David and Goliath would have taught us anything if David would have been as big as Goliath?

LET'S DO!

King Saul wanted David to wear the royal war armor before meeting Goliath. David probably looked silly wearing the armor that was made for grown-up King Saul because David himself was just a small child. Today, let's play dress up! Parents, provide the children with large clothing and shoes to put on, just as David put on King Saul's armor. Then, have them do tasks or activities around the house that might be difficult to do while wearing clothing not meant for them. After doing the household tasks, talk about what it might have been like for David to walk around as a child in King Saul's war armor, wearing heavy gear on his body and a helmet that covered his eyes! Remember that it's part of God's plan for us to grow into these clothes (or armor) throughout our lives, both physically and spiritually.

Father, we thank You for the story of David and Goliath. Thank You for using David even though he was young and small. Help us remember that You have plans to use us no matter how young or old or how small or large we may be. Amen.

STAND UP

For if you remain silent at this time, relief and deliverance
for the Jews will arise from another place, but you and your
father's family will perish. And who knows but that you have
come to your royal position for such a time as this?

—ESTHER 4:14

Today, we are going to learn about a young woman in the Bible who was courageous. She did
something brave to save people, even though she didn't have to. Esther was young when she
became a queen. Her husband, the king of Persia, had a right-hand man named Haman who did
not like the Jewish people. In fact, he disliked them so much that he made a plot to kill them.

What Haman and the king didn't know was that Queen Esther was Jewish. Haman was
plotting to kill the queen's own people! Mordechai, a relative of Queen Esther, urged her to tell
the king what Haman was up to. At first, she was afraid. But she knew she had to do the right
thing, reveal she was Jewish, and stand up for her people. Esther could have stayed silent. She
could have let the fear quiet her and stay in hiding. But she had courage and trusted in God. By
telling the king her own truth and the truth of Haman's plans, she saved her people.

Sometimes it is hard and even scary to stand up for the right thing. Yet, staying silent can
bring harm to others and sometimes even ourselves. When we are standing up for what is right,
we can be sure that God is by our side and protecting us.

LET'S REFLECT!

1. Haman was a bully. Have you ever faced a bully?
2. What does bullying look like to you? How can you stand up to a bully?

*Parents, the topic of bullies can be hard. Today, really listen to what your kids are saying.

LET'S DO!

Queen Esther had to be brave to save her people. Likewise, we need to be brave to stand up for what is right. Let's practice being brave today with something very fun and very yummy. We are going to make snow cones! Gather ice, a baggie, a hammer, and cups. Put ice into a baggie and using the hammer, carefully crush the ice. Make sure each person gets a chance to crush the ice. Pour the crushed ice into cups. Next, pour juice over the ice. Here is the brave, yet fun part. Use a flavor you wouldn't normally choose. Try something new!

Father, help us to stand up for what is right and for those who need us, even when it is hard. Help us remember to use kind words and show love. Amen.

TALKING WITH GOD

Now when Daniel learned that the decree had been published, he went home to his upstairs room where the windows opened toward Jerusalem. Three times a day he got down on his knees and prayed, giving thanks to his God, just as he had done before.

—DANIEL 6:10

Does praying every day seem hard? Is it difficult to think of what to say or hard talking to someone you can't see? Should you close your eyes or not? What should you do with your hands? Praying doesn't have to be hard or confusing! Prayer is an important part of a Christian's life and something we should do every day.

In Daniel, we read about Daniel's prayer life. Daniel prayed to God three times every day. Even when King Darius made a law that no one could pray, Daniel still prayed! He knew how important prayer was. He knew that by praying, he was talking to God and growing his relationship with God.

You see, that is what prayer is—it is simply talking to God. It doesn't have to be filled with fancy words. It doesn't have to be hard or uncomfortable. You don't have to close your eyes and fold your hands, though doing so helps to keep yourself focused on praying. God loves when we pray. He loves when we thank Him, when we worship Him, when we tell Him how we're feeling, and when we ask Him for help.

LET'S REFLECT!

1. Do you struggle to pray every day? Does it feel weird or uncomfortable?

2. The more we pray, the closer we grow to God and the easier prayer becomes. Talk about having a prayer time each day.

LET'S DO!

Sometimes when we pray, we aren't sure what to pray for. Today, we are going to create a Five Finger Prayer. Gather paper and crayons or markers. Have each person trace their hand on a piece of paper. On each finger, write out something you can pray for. For example, you could write family, friends, country, neighbors, and yourself. After each person decides what they want to add to their hand, cut the hands out. You can keep your hands on the refrigerator, taped to your mirror, or in your Bible. Whenever you pray, use your hand to remind you what you want to pray for.

Father, thank You for giving prayer to us as a way to talk with You. Help us remember how important prayer is and that it doesn't have to be hard. Amen.

WORSHIP GOD ALONE

Then King Nebuchadnezzar leaped to his feet in amazement and asked his advisers, "Weren't there three men that we tied up and threw into the fire?" They replied, "Certainly, Your Majesty." He said, "Look! I see four men walking around in the fire, unbound and unharmed, and the fourth looks like a son of the gods."

—DANIEL 3:24–25

Shadrach, Meshach, and Abednego learned a big lesson in worshipping only God. The men loved and worshipped God. But King Nebuchadnezzar wanted the people to worship him. He made a golden statue of himself and whenever the music would play, the people were to bow down and worship his golden statue. King Nebuchadnezzar was pretty full of himself!

Shadrach, Meshach, and Abednego knew that bowing to anyone other than God was wrong, so they refused to bow down to the golden statue. This made King Nebuchadnezzar very angry. He was so angry that he tied the men up and threw them into a fiery furnace. He was trying to kill them because they wouldn't worship him! But when the king looked into the furnace, he didn't see three men, he saw four! The Lord was with the men and had protected them from the fire. They came out unhurt and didn't even smell like smoke.

We are called to worship God and only God. We are not to worship any other person or thing. We need to put God first in our life, above all other people and all things.

LET'S REFLECT!

1. Do you put anyone in your life before God? Maybe a super-hero or celebrity? What about things? Do you put your gaming system or other material things before God?

2. Discuss the ways in which putting God first is actually the most rewarding relationship of all.

LET'S DO!

King Nebuchadnezzar put Shadrach, Meshach, and Abednego into a fiery furnace and made the furnace seven times hotter than normal. Fire can be very dangerous. If we are not safe and fail to have safe boundaries, fire can hurt us badly. But there is one thing fire is fun for—if we are careful and are with an adult—and that is s'mores! Today, gather all the delicious ingredients for s'mores, then build a safe fire (grown-ups, this is your job!). As you sit around your fire and roast marsh-mallows for a yummy treat, read the full story of Shadrach, Meshach, and Abednego from Daniel 3. Then take turns talking about how we are called by God to worship only Him.

Father, thank You for the story of Shadrach, Meshach, and Abednego. Thank You for showing us that these men stood strong and only worshipped You. Help us to follow their example and worship You alone. Amen.

FISHING FOR GUIDANCE

Jonah obeyed the word of the Lord and went to Nineveh.
Now Nineveh was a very large city; it took three days to go
through it.

—JONAH 3:3

Following the rules isn't always easy. Someone—a parent, teacher, boss, anyone in authority over us—tells us to do something and if we don't want to do it, we start thinking of a way to get out of it. Jonah learned the hard way that it is easier and wiser to just listen!

God wanted Jonah to go to Nineveh to preach to the wicked people. He didn't think the people would listen to him because he knew how evil they were. So instead of going to Nineveh, he got on a ship and went the opposite way. God needed to get Jonah's attention and teach him a lesson, so He sent a big storm. The storm was so bad that everyone on the ship thought they were going to die. When they found out Jonah was running from God, they threw him into the sea! But God wasn't done with Jonah. He sent a big fish to swallow Jonah whole.

When Jonah was in the big fish, he realized that by disobeying God's order, he was sinning. He asked God to forgive him. Three days later the fish spit Jonah up onto the shore. Jonah went to Nineveh and preached to the people.

LET'S REFLECT!

1. Do you find it easy to always follow the rules?

2. If Jonah had followed God's guidance in the beginning, he wouldn't have spent three days in the belly of a fish. Think of a time you could have avoided trouble if you had just listened.

LET'S DO!

Jonah was swallowed whole by a big fish. Can you imagine spending three days inside the belly of a giant fish? Today, let's go fishing! If you enjoy the great outdoors, take a family trip to a lake or a pond and enjoy some time fishing. (Don't worry! These fish won't swallow you whole!) If you prefer the cozy indoors, make a fishing pole by taking a broomstick and taping string to one end. On the opposite end of the string, attach a paperclip or clothespin. Then gather some treats—candy, stickers, coins, etc. Put a blanket on the ground, with the treats on one side and the fishermen on the other. Cast your line over the blanket and fish for a treat.

Father, thank You for giving us people in authority over us. It isn't always easy to obey. Help us to obey those You have given to us and You. Amen.

RESOLVING CONFLICTS

If your brother or sister sins, go and point out their fault, just between the two of you. If they listen to you, you have won them over.

—MATTHEW 18:15

Do you always get along with everyone? Probably not! We all have conflicts from time to time. We don't get along with every person all the time. We will disagree with people occasionally. Even people we love, even with people we enjoy being with. You will even disagree with family!

How can we resolve our conflict in a way that honors God? We need to remain calm when we get angry; if we let our emotions take control, we can cause more damage. Jesus tells us in Matthew that we should go to the person we have a problem with and try to talk it out, try to point out what they did wrong. But we also need to listen to them—because maybe we have done something wrong, too. If we calmly talk one-on-one with the person, each person listening to each other, oftentimes we can resolve the problem quickly. If they won't listen, go to another person like a parent, explain the situation, and ask them to mediate—to go between the two of you to help straighten it out.

It is important to ask forgiveness if you have hurt or offended the other person. It is just as important to forgive them. When we follow this method for resolving conflict, we can honor God and save our relationships.

LET'S REFLECT!

1. Think of some of the relationships you have: your siblings, your neighbors, your friends. Do you always get along with these people?

2. When we calmly talk and carefully listen to the person we are having an issue with, we can often fix the problem quickly. Discuss what it would look like to do this.

LET'S DO!

Today, we are going to play a game called Snowman. Ask an adult to make a list of words on a sheet of paper that can be used when resolving conflict (i.e., understanding, forgiveness, etc.). Cut the list of words into strips, fold the strips, place them in a bowl, and pick a word. Set up your game using a board or paper. One person draws while everybody else guesses letters to try and find the chosen word. For every incorrect guess, the person draws another segment of the snowman, going from bottom to top. You can add a face, carrot nose, top hat, and anything else you like! After each round, discuss what the words have to do with resolving conflict, and how we can keep our cool and honor God and, at the same time, solve our problems with each other.

Father, thank You for giving us a way to resolve our problems with each other. Help us to always be willing to work out our problems and honor You. Amen.

CHILDREN ARE SPECIAL

Jesus said, "Let the little children come to me, and do not hinder them, for the kingdom of heaven belongs to such as these."

—MATTHEW 19:14

Children are special to Jesus. One day people were taking their children to Jesus, and He was placing His hands on each one and praying for them. But Jesus's disciples thought it was a waste of time. They thought Jesus should be focusing on the adults and the sick. They thought the children were bothering Jesus. But Jesus rebuked them ("rebuked" is another word for "corrected"). Jesus wanted the children to come to Him. Jesus even told the disciples to let the children come. Heaven belonged to them!

Children have a pure faith that adults sometimes forget about. Children trust their parents will protect them and take care of them. They trust their parents love them and will be there for them. Jesus wants adults to learn from the children and have pure faith in Him. He wants everyone to know how much He loves them and that He will always be there for them, protect them, and take care of them.

No matter how young or how old you are, Jesus wants you to place your trust in Him just like a child places trust in their parent.

LET'S REFLECT!

1. Children, do you trust your parents to always take care of you and be there? Do you trust God in the same way? Why or why not?

2. Parents, do you remember when you placed complete trust in someone? Do you trust God in the same way? Why or why not?

LET'S DO!

Having faith and trust in Jesus means knowing that even though we can't see what is coming, we know He is in control, and He will take care of us. Today, we are going to play a trust game! Set up an obstacle course using pillows and blankets and divide up into pairs. Blindfold one person in each pair and have their buddy hold their hand to lead them through the obstacle course. They will have to trust their buddy to lead them through the course safely. Once they are done, they can swap places, so everyone gets a turn. After every person has gone through the course blindfolded, talk together about what it means to trust in Jesus.

Father, thank You for teaching us that children are special and that we—no matter our age—should trust in You like children. Amen.

CHRISTMAS ALL YEAR LONG

Today in the town of David a Savior has been born to you; he is the Messiah, the Lord. This will be a sign to you: You will find a baby wrapped in cloths and lying in a manger.

—LUKE 2:11–12

Christmas is such a beautiful time of year! We have lights, decorations, special cookies, Christmas movies, hot cocoa, festive pajamas, music, fun parties, and much more. For one month—or maybe a little longer—we enjoy all the goodness of the Christmas season.

Throughout the time of Christmas, we hear many people say, "Jesus is the reason for the season." But do we really believe that? Do we really believe that Jesus is the true reason for Christmas? If we do believe that Jesus is the reason, then we know the season isn't just one month long. Instead, we know that Christmas is all year long!

God sent His Son to save us from our sins and give us a hope and a future with Him in heaven. This gift from God is not just for December. It is for every day. We can celebrate Christmas all year long by living for God and serving Him.

LET'S REFLECT!

1. What do you believe is the meaning of Christmas and why?

2. What do you think Christmas might look like if we celebrated the true meaning of Jesus?

LET'S DO!

No matter what the date is on the calendar, we are going to celebrate the real Christmas today! Pick one or two of your family's favorite Christmas traditions, like wearing your favorite Christmas pajamas, baking some Christmas treats, singing Christmas carols, watching a Christmas movie, or reading the story of the birth of Jesus in the Bible. After enjoying your holiday fun, talk about the true meaning of Christmas—the coming of Jesus to save us from our sins—and how you can enjoy and honor the gift of Jesus all year long.

Father, thank You for sending us a Christmas gift to last all year long! Help us remember the true meaning of Christmas and how we can celebrate it every day. Amen.

LET'S USE OUR HELPING HANDS

He answered, "Love the Lord your God with all your heart and with all your soul and with all your strength and with all your mind"; and, "Love your neighbor as yourself."

—LUKE 10:27

In Luke, Jesus tells the story of a Levite man who was robbed and beaten up when he was traveling. Pretty soon a priest walked by. You would think the priest would help the man, but he didn't! He went to the other side of the road to stay away from him. Then another Levite man walked by. Being a fellow Levite, you would think he would help, but he didn't either!

Then, a Samaritan man walked by. Now Levites and Samaritans didn't like each other very much. But the Samaritan could see that the man was alone, hurting, and in need of help. So, he used his helping hands to clean the man's cuts and then took him to town to be cared for.

It is important to help others. There are lots of ways we can help people every day, even our own family. And when we use our helping hands, we make God smile!

LET'S REFLECT!

1. Why do you think the first two men didn't help the hurt man? Why do you think the Samaritan man helped?

2. Think of ways you can use your helping hands.

LET'S DO!

No matter how young or old you are, everyone can be a helper. Today, we are going to work as a team to help. Visit an elderly family member or neighbor and help do work around their house. You can do things like rake the leaves, mow the lawn, take out the trash, do the dishes, and vacuum the carpet. Sometimes these things can be harder for someone who is elderly, but when you work together as a family and team, you can get it done in no time! After you help, sit and talk with them. Spending time with people is also a way to help.

Father, thank You for the story of the Good Samaritan. Help us be good helpers and help other people and each other. Amen.

FIGHTING TEMPTATION LIKE JESUS

Jesus said to him, "Away from Me, Satan! For it is written:
'Worship the Lord your God, and serve Him only.'"

—MATTHEW 4:10

Are you ever tempted to do something you know you shouldn't? Temptation is around us every single day. We are tempted to tell a fib in an attempt to stay out of trouble. We are tempted to skimp on our chores when we know we should do them correctly. We are tempted to eat more cookies than we are allowed to. Yes, temptation hits everyone.

Did you know that Jesus was tempted too? The Bible tells us in Matthew 4 that Jesus had been fasting for forty days. Can you imagine not eating anything for forty days? After the forty days, Satan took Jesus into the wilderness and tempted Him to turn the rocks into bread so He could eat. Then, Satan tempted Jesus to jump off the highest point, saying the angels would save Him. And finally, Satan tempted Jesus by telling Him if He bowed down to Satan, He could have all the kingdoms of the world. But every time Satan tried to tempt Jesus, Jesus fought back with words from the Bible!

We can fight temptation just like Jesus. When we are tempted to do something we know we should not do, we can remember what the Bible says.

LET'S REFLECT!

1. What are some of your temptations?
2. What can you do when you feel tempted?

LET'S DO!

Jesus didn't fight Satan and temptation on His own. He used the words from the Bible. Today, we are going to do the same. Gather a Bible, one piece of paper per person, and pens. Have each person make a list of two or three things they are often tempted to do. Next, as a family, look up Bible verses that can help you fight that temptation. You can use the concordance in the back of your Bible, the YouVersion Bible app, or Biblestudytools.com to help you. Write the verse next to your temptation. After everyone has their temptation and verses, talk about how Jesus fought temptation and how we can fight like Him.

Father, thank You for fighting against the enemy and against temptation and for showing us how we can fight, too. Help us remember to use the Bible and stand strong. Amen.

BEAUTY IN DIFFERENCES

The Samaritan woman said to him, "You are a Jew and I am a Samaritan woman. How can you ask me for a drink?" (For Jews do not associate with Samaritans.)

—JOHN 4:9

If you look around this world, you will see people of all shapes and sizes, of all colors and backgrounds. Sometimes it can be overwhelming, but it doesn't have to be. There is beauty in all our differences. God created each and every person, and He made us different on purpose.

In John, the Bible tells us a story of Jesus, who was a Jew, encountering someone who was different from Him. When He was sitting by a well, a Samaritan woman walked by. The Jews and Samaritans did not like each other. Jesus asked the woman for a drink of water from the well. The woman was shocked that Jesus was talking to her. You see, Jesus didn't care that she was a Samaritan. He saw the beauty in their differences and knew that if she would just talk to Him, to Jesus, He could help her.

When we look at people who are different from us, we shouldn't be scared or angry or unsure. We should notice the beauty and thank God that He made each person to be different. What a boring world it would be if we were all the same!

LET'S REFLECT!

1. Why do you think the Samaritan woman was surprised Jesus was talking to her?

2. There are many different shapes, sizes, skin colors, and backgrounds. The differences are beautiful, created on purpose by God. Think of someone you know that looks different from you. How can you celebrate your differences? What are the ways in which you are the same?

LET'S DO!

Color is beautiful! God gave us a rainbow of colors like red, blue, green, and so many more. He also gave us a rainbow of people, a beautiful rainbow. Today, as a family, make a wreath of hands! Gather paper, scissors, tape or glue, and crayons. Trace five to ten hands on the pieces of paper. Color each hand a different skin color. Cut the hands out and place them in a circle as a wreath. Go from the lightest to the darkest color. Tape or glue the hands together making a beautiful wreath. Finish today's activity by talking about how beautiful our differences are.

Father, thank You for our differences! You made each and every person different, and it is a beautiful rainbow. Help us remember that You created each person. Amen.

PEACE BE STILL

He replied, "You of little faith, why are you so afraid?" Then He got up and rebuked the winds and the waves, and it was completely calm.

—MATTHEW 8:26

Do you ever get afraid? Everyone does. In Matthew, the Bible tells us a story of when the disciples were afraid. Jesus and his disciples were at sea on a boat when a big storm came up. The giant waves were crashing against the boat, and the men feared they would sink. All the while, Jesus slept!

The men were so afraid they woke Jesus up and begged Him to save them. Jesus asked them why they were so afraid. The disciples had more fear of the storm than they had trust in Jesus. Jesus told the wind and waves to stop, and they did! Yet, even if Jesus had not calmed the storm, they still could have trusted in Jesus because He is more powerful than the storm.

Sometimes we encounter things in life that are scary. Maybe it is a storm like the disciples faced, maybe a scary-looking spider, or maybe a bully. No matter what it is we face, we can trust that Jesus will be with us.

LET'S REFLECT!

1. What is something scary you have recently faced?
2. What can you do to remind yourself to trust in Jesus when the scary things in life arise?

LET'S DO!

In your Bibles, read Matthew 8:23–27. Next, create a makeshift boat. You can use a box, plastic swimming pool, laundry basket, or anything of the like. Use a fan or hairdryer to be the wind. Act out Matthew 8:23–27, and give each person a chance to play Jesus and tell the wind and waves to obey. After, sit down and talk about things that might be scary and how we can trust in Jesus even in the scary moments of life. Make sure everyone gets a chance to share openly about their fears, without any judgment. And finally, pray together asking Jesus to help you trust in Him with what scares you.

Father, thank You for always being there to protect us. Help us remember that You are far more powerful than anything we will ever face. Amen.

WHO YOU SURROUND YOURSELF WITH MATTERS

Since they could not get him to Jesus because of the crowd, they made an opening in the roof above Jesus by digging through it and then lowered the mat the man was lying on.

—MARK 2:4

Friends are important! We need people in our life that we can laugh with, play with, cry with, and talk to. But who those friends are matters. The Bible tells us of a man who was paralyzed and couldn't walk. His friends heard that Jesus was nearby, so they decided to take their friend to Jesus.

The men put their friend on a blanket, and each held a corner. They carried their friend all the way to Jesus. No car. No wagon. Just men walking on foot. When they got to the house where Jesus was, they saw it was so full they couldn't get inside. So, they went to the roof and carefully lowered the man on the blanket down to the feet of Jesus. Because of the man's faith, and the faith of his friends, Jesus healed him and forgave his sins.

We need to have friends that carry us to Jesus. Friends who pray for us. Friends who will encourage us to read the Bible and go to church. Friends who don't try to get us to do things that are wrong. We need to surround ourselves with friends who take us to Jesus.

LET'S REFLECT!

1. Do you have any friends who influence you to do things you know are wrong? Are you the kind of friend who is a bad influence, or are you the friend who carries your friends to Jesus?

2. Parents and guardians, remember to explain that it is possible to have good, kind friends who may be of a different faith. Discuss why it is a good thing to have friends with different beliefs and perspectives.

LET'S DO!

It is important to have good friends—friends who are there for us and take us to Jesus. When we have these good friends, we need to cultivate and grow those relationships. Today, make a plan to hang out with friends. You could schedule a day at the park, a dinner at home, or any other activity you enjoy together. However, if you don't have a Godly friend, now is a great time to start praying as a family that God will bring good Godly friends into your lives.

Father, thank You for good friends who take us to You. Help us surround ourselves with good friends and to cultivate those friendships. Amen.

GIVE THANKS

One of them, when he saw he was healed, came back, praising God in a loud voice. He threw himself at Jesus's feet and thanked him—and he was a Samaritan.

—LUKE 17:15–16

It is important to say "thank you." One man in the Bible knew this. There were ten men who had a contagious and incurable disease called leprosy. Jesus saw the ten men and told them to go show themselves to the priest, and they would be healed. One man went back to Jesus and said, "thank you." There were ten and only one went back and gave thanks.

We need to learn from the man who went back to Jesus and say "thank you" often. There is so much we can say "thank you" for! Kids can thank their parents for taking care of them and for the little things they do for you. Parents can thank kids for listening and helping.

And we should always thank Jesus. We need to thank Him for all the blessings He has given us, for taking care of us each day, and healing us. We need to thank Him for the people He has given us, the food we eat, and our home. There is so much to thank Jesus for!

LET'S REFLECT!

1. Is saying "thank you" easy for you? If not, why do you think that is?

2. Have everyone finish this sentence: Jesus, thank You for
_____.

LET'S DO!

Saying "thank you" is important, for kids and adults. Today, we are going to say "thank you" to a group of people in a very special way. We are going to bake some delicious cookies together as a family and deliver them to first responders—police officers, firefighters, EMTs, and frontline healthcare workers! Be sure to use those two special words—thank you—every chance you get! While your cookies are cooling, write out a thank you card. Thank the first responders for their service to your community. Once your cookies are ready, wrap them up and place the card with them. Pray over the cookies, asking God to protect your first responders. Then, deliver your cookies and card to your first responders. Be sure to thank them!

Father, thank You for all Your blessings! Help us remember the importance of thanking others. Help those two words, thank you, to be a regular part of our speech. Amen.

KEEP YOUR EYES ON JESUS

"Come," He said. Then Peter got down out of the boat, walked on the water and came toward Jesus. But when he saw the wind, he was afraid and, beginning to sink, cried out, "Lord, save me!"

—MATTHEW 14:29–30

The disciples were out on the sea floating along in their boat, when suddenly they saw someone walking on top of the water! They thought it was a ghost! But it wasn't a ghost at all. It was Jesus. Jesus called out to reassure them it was Him. Peter decided he needed more convincing and told Jesus, "Lord, if it's You, tell me to come to You on the water." Jesus told Peter to walk out to Him.

Peter stepped out of the boat and began walking on the water toward Jesus. Amazing! But when Peter saw the wind, he became afraid—after all, walking on the water isn't normal. When Peter took his eyes off Jesus, he sank, and Jesus had to save him.

When we keep our eyes fixed on Jesus, we can face all that comes our way. But when we take our eyes off Jesus, we will sink. We must trust in Jesus and know that He will take care of us no matter what happens. When we trust in Jesus, we can keep our eyes firmly fixed on Him.

LET'S REFLECT!

1. How do you think you'd respond if you were in a boat in the middle of the water and saw someone walking on top of the water?

2. Peter learned the importance of keeping his eyes on Jesus. What does this look like to you?

LET'S DO!

Jesus walked on the water, and while he kept his eyes on Jesus, Peter walked on the water, too. To celebrate their amazing feat, today we are going to have some fun with water! Grab some water balloons and fill them with water. Go outside, divide into two teams, and have a water balloon fight. If weather does not permit, divide into two teams. Each team will create a mini boat with things from around the house. You can fold one out of paper, make one out of popsicle sticks, or use anything else that floats. Then using a long bucket or the bathtub, have boat races. When you are done with your water balloon fight or boat races, talk about what it means to keep our eyes on Jesus and trust Him.

Father, thank You for always being Someone we can trust. Help us keep our eyes firmly fixed on You and to know that no matter what we face, You will always be there. Amen.

SWEET HONEY

Gracious words are a honeycomb, sweet to the soul and healing to the bones.

—PROVERBS 16:24

Do you like honey? Honey is tasty on top of a warm biscuit, in a cup of tea, or glazed over fruit. Honey is so sweet and so good, that the Bible tells us in Proverbs that our words should be like honey.

The words we say and the way we speak matters. Proverbs 18:21 even tells us that our words have the power of life and death. That is pretty important! Your words can help someone feel better and encourage them. And your words can hurt and bring someone down.

We need to be careful with the words we say. Before we speak, we should really think about what we are saying. Are our words true, helpful, important, necessary, and kind? If not, maybe we shouldn't be saying them. We also need to watch the tone we use. If your words are kind but your tone is rude, your words will still sound unkind. Are we speaking in a way that is kind and respectful, or are we speaking in a way that is rude and hurtful? Let's make sure our words are sweet like honey!

LET'S REFLECT!

1. What words you use and how you say them make a difference. How do you feel when someone speaks kindly to you? How do you feel when they are rude?

2. We should be careful not to say words that are inappropriate, rude, or hurtful. How can you make your words sweet today?

LET'S DO!

Today, we are going to make a kindness jar. You will need a clear jar, such as a Mason jar or clear pitcher, pebbles or marbles, a bowl or second jar to hold your pebbles or marbles, a piece of paper for a label, a marker, and tape. On your paper, write the word KINDNESS. Tape the paper to your jar. Next, talk about kind words, letting everyone have a chance to share. Talk about words that are kind and words that are unkind. Over the next month or so, every time someone uses a kind word, add a pebble or marble to the kindness jar. Once your kindness jar is full, have a family fun day to celebrate!

Father, thank You for teaching us to have sweet words. Help us remember to watch the words we say and the tone we use. Help us bring life with our words. Amen.

BEING LAST IS OKAY

But many who are first will be last, and the last first.

—MARK 10:31

Who doesn't like to be first? When we are first, we get to pick the best seat, the freshest food, our favorite toy, our choice of TV show. However, the Bible gives us a different look at being first.

The Bible tells us we don't always have to be first. It even says, the first will be last and the last first. That sounds crazy! How can we be first if we are last? When we let others go ahead of us, we are being humble, kind, and patient. Jesus loves when we are humble, kind, and patient. When we show these characteristics, it makes Him happy, and He will honor these traits. But when we rush to be first, we are showing selfishness, and this makes Jesus sad. He doesn't want us to be selfish and always thinking of ourselves.

Jesus wants us to be humble, kind, and patient. And when we are, we don't mind being last, because we know that we are pleasing Jesus.

LET'S REFLECT!

1. Is waiting hard for you? Why or why not?

2. Think of a time you let someone go in front of you. How did it make you feel knowing you were being kind and patient?

LET'S DO!

Games are lots of fun, but everyone can't always play at the same time. When we play games, we must show patience as we wait for our turn. Today, let's have a game day! Grab your favorite snacks and your favorite game. It could be a video game, board game, or card game. Make sure you take turns, play fair, and be patient as you wait your turn. And don't forget to cheer each other on! This is a great way to practice our patience and kindness when we let others go first.

Father, thank You for teaching us that we don't always have to be first. Help us show humility, kindness, and patience as we let others go first and wait our turn. Amen.

GIVE FROM THE HEART

All these people gave their gifts out of their wealth; but she out of her poverty put in all she had to live on.

—LUKE 21:4

Jesus told a parable—a story—about giving. Some rich folks gave large amounts of money as an offering at the temple, but because they were rich, it wasn't a sacrifice or a big deal to them. Then a widow came in and gave two small coins. It was all she had.

Jesus asked who gave more, the rich people or the poor widow. You would think the rich people gave more. What they put into the offering was a much larger amount than the widow who only gave two small coins. But Jesus said the widow gave more! How is that possible? It's because the widow gave everything she had, and she gave from her heart.

When we give, we need to give from our heart. When we give our offering at church, we shouldn't think of other ways we could spend the money or wish we could keep it. We should joyfully give—whether sharing a cookie with a friend, giving a gift, or helping a neighbor. We should never give with grudge or bad attitude; we should be happy to give.

LET'S REFLECT!

1. Why do you think we give an offering at church?
2. What does it mean to you when we say "give with a joyful heart"?

LET'S DO!

Another way to give from the heart is to help those in need. As a family, brainstorm ways you can help someone this week. These ideas might include serving food in a soup kitchen, making sack lunches to give to homeless people, visiting a nursing home, or helping an elderly relative or neighbor. What are other ideas you can think of to help someone? Make a list of everyone's ideas, then vote on what you will do as a family. Once you have your idea, make a plan, and then do it. Just be sure you are serving with a joyful heart.

Father, thank You for the lesson to give with our all and with a joyful heart. Help us joyfully give our offering to You and serve others. Amen.

HEAVEN BOUND

For God so loved the world that He gave His one and only Son, that whoever believes in Him shall not perish but have eternal life.

—JOHN 3:16

Have you ever wondered what it takes to get to heaven? There was a man in the Bible who wondered this too. Nicodemus wanted to know what it took to get to heaven, so late one night he went to see Jesus and asked Him.

Jesus told Nicodemus that God sent Him to this world so we could one day go to heaven. He told Nicodemus exactly what he had to do to get there: believe.

God loves every single person in the world so much that He sent His only Son, Jesus, to this world to die for our sins and rise again, so that one day we could live in heaven with Him. All we must do is admit our sins, acknowledge that we need Jesus, believe in Him, and publicly confess our belief in Him. That is all it takes to be heaven bound!

LET'S REFLECT!

1. John 3:16 says God sent Jesus for whoever believes in Him. That means you, if you believe.

2. Parents and guardians, do you remember when you asked Jesus into your heart? If so, think on that time and share how special you felt. If not, are you ready to do so now?

LET'S DO!

John 3:16 is the very center of the Gospel of Jesus. This one verse is powerful, telling the world how they can be heaven bound. Today, let's work on memorizing these words! Sit or stand in a circle. Have the first person say the word "For" from John 3:16. Go around the circle, with the next person saying the next word of the verse. Continue until you've said all of John 3:16. Do this a few times, trying not to look at the words. After you've done the entire verse a few times, talk about the ABCs of salvation: Admit you sin, Believe in Jesus as your Savior, and Confess your belief. If anyone hasn't asked Jesus into their heart, now is a great time to say that prayer if they are ready.

Father, thank You for sending Your Son Jesus to this world to save us from our sins. Help us live for You in all that we do, say, and think. Amen.

ONE WAY

Jesus answered, "I am the way and the truth and the life. No one comes to the Father except through Me."

—JOHN 14:6

In John, we are told that the only way to God the Father is through His Son, Jesus.

Some people will tell you different ways to get to God, such as helping the needy, going to church every week, giving in offering, reading the Bible, not cursing, and not lying. These are all important things. It is important to help the needy, go to church, give offering, and read the Bible. These are things we should want to *do!* And it is important to avoid saying curse words or lying. But those things in themselves will not get you to God.

The only way to God is through Jesus. We must admit we sin, know that we need Jesus, believe He came to this world to die for our sins and rise again, and confess that He is Lord. We must remember that to truly get to God, there is only one way—through Jesus.

LET'S REFLECT!

1. Think about all the things we should do as Christians, such as going to church, reading our Bible, doing good things, and giving offering. What are some examples of Christian things we do every day? Sharing toys? Listening quietly? What else can you add?

2. Even though we should do all those things, the only way to get to God, or to heaven, is through Jesus Christ. Have you accepted Him into your heart?

LET'S DO!

John 3:16 and John 14:6 are the roots of the Gospel of Jesus. They tell us that God loved us so much He sent His own Son to this Earth to die on the cross and rise again so that we can, through Him, get to God. Today, let's make roots of another kind! Gather seeds of any kind from a fruit or vegetable or even a pack of seeds, cups or small planting pots for each person, and dirt. Add a little dirt to your pot, sprinkle in your seeds, add some more dirt, then water your seeds. Place your cups or planting pots where they will feel God's warmth and the sun for the next few weeks. Watch your seeds take root and sprout.

Father, thank You for sending Your Son Jesus to be the way to You. Help us remember that He is the only way, and when we live for Him, we will find You. Amen.

SHARING WHAT WE HAVE

Here is a boy with five small barley loaves and two small fish, but how far will they go among so many?

—JOHN 6:9

Sharing what we have isn't always easy. Especially if we only have a little bit. But one boy in the Bible learned how sharing what you have with others can make a big impact!

Jesus was preaching to more than five thousand men, women, and children. The people had been there all day and were getting hungry. They couldn't order a pizza or run to the drive-thru. To get food, they were going to have to walk a very long way, and they were tired and hungry. But Jesus had a plan!

There was a little boy who had two fish and five loaves of bread. That was his food for the day. But the little boy offered his food to Jesus. Now think about this. There were five thousand men. Plus, there were many women and children. And all they had were two fish and five loaves of bread. It doesn't sound like it would be enough, does it?

Jesus blessed the food and the disciples started to hand it out. Guess what? Suddenly there was much more food than before. They were able to feed everyone there, *and* they had leftovers!

LET'S REFLECT!

1. Think about the boy who shared his fish and bread. Do you think that was hard for him? Or do you think he trusted Jesus?

2. Think about a time you had to share something. Was that hard for you to do? Why or why not?

LET'S DO!

There are a lot of people in this world who are hungry. Maybe they don't have any food at all, or maybe they just don't have enough food; either way, they are hungry. Today, let's feed them. Make some sack lunches. You could add peanut butter and jelly sandwiches, a few chips, and even a cookie. It doesn't matter if you make five sack lunches or fifty sack lunches. Anything helps. Remember, the boy only had two fish and five loaves of bread. Pray over your sack lunches, then deliver them to homeless people or families in need. Want to make an even bigger impact? Ask a few other families to help! The more people who make sack lunches, the more people you can feed!

Father, thank You for seeing when we share. Help us remember to share, no matter how big or small it is, because we know You will bless it. Amen.

BE PATIENT

Be completely humble and gentle; be patient, bearing with one another in love.

—EPHESIANS 4:2

Being patient is hard. It isn't easy to wait, especially if it is for something we really want. Sometimes, we have to wait to eat when we are hungry. We must wait for our favorite TV show to come on or a new movie to come out. We must wait for our favorite holiday or birthday. We must wait at the doctor's office. We must wait for the ooey-gooey cookies to come out of the oven and cool off before we can eat them. There is just so much to wait and be patient for. It is so hard!

However, being patient is important. We will have to wait for an abundance of things throughout our lives, so we must learn how to be patient. Sometimes waiting makes us upset or anxious. The Bible tells us to be humble, gentle, and patient. We can do this by remembering that sometimes things take time. If we rush our dinner, it might not get cooked properly. If we don't wait our turn for the TV or our favorite toy, then someone else will be deprived of what they already had. If we don't wait for the cookies to cool, we could burn our tongue. Waiting isn't easy, but the more we practice patience, the better we get it at it.

LET'S REFLECT!

1.   What is something you have a hard time being patient for?
2.   How can you practice having patience?

LET'S DO!

To be patient, we need to slow down and understand that things take time, and that is okay. Let's practice slowing down and being patient today with a fun game. This game will be best done outside or on a hard floor. Make a start line on one side of the room and a finish line on the other side or about eight feet away. Give everyone a spoon and an egg. Divide into pairs, each pair will race against the other. Have the first player from each team stand at the starting line, holding the spoon in one hand. Place an egg on each player's spoon. When you say "Begin!" each player should carefully and patiently walk to the finish line. The first one there without dropping their egg wins! Continue to play until you have one grand champion.

Father, thank You for teaching us to be patient. Help us remember that sometimes we need to slow down, wait, and be patient. Help us show patience in all we do. Amen.

PUT ON THE ARMOR

Put on the full armor of God, so that you can take your stand against the devil's schemes.

—EPHESIANS 6:11

Have you ever watched a football game where the players didn't wear pads? Have you ever watched a hockey game where the players didn't wear a mouth guard? Have you ever watched a baseball game where the batter didn't wear a batting helmet? You probably answered "No" to all these questions. Some athletes wear protective gear when they are going to play their sport to protect themselves. It is important to keep their bodies safe.

In the same way, we need to put on the full armor of God to protect ourselves. An enemy who doesn't want us to live for God is very real. We need to be on the lookout for temptation and sin, which comes from Satan. But when we have the full armor of God on—the belt of truth, the breastplate of righteousness, the gospel shoes of peace, the shield of faith, the helmet of salvation, and the Sword of the Spirit—we are protected! The enemy will still scheme and throw his arrows at us, but we are covered!

LET'S REFLECT!

1. Think of a time you played or watched a sport. Did you or the players have to put on protective gear? Why?

2. Think about the pieces of the armor of God. Discuss what each piece means and how you can "put on the armor" each day.

LET'S DO!

Family sports can be so fun! You get quality time together, you get to move your body and be active, and you get some sunshine. Today, let's play a sport together. Take a family vote on which sport you will do. Just remember, the losing votes cannot get upset. You will have so much fun no matter what you play. Then go into the yard or to the park and have an active and fun game of whatever sport you choose. You can also call up another family and make it a family-on-family competition. Don't forget to put on your protective gear!

Father, thank You for the armor that protects us. Help us remember how important it is to put on the full armor of God every single day to protect ourselves against the enemy. Amen.

NOT ASHAMED

For I am not ashamed of the gospel, because it is the power of God that brings salvation to everyone who believes: first to the Jew, then to the Gentile.

—ROMANS 1:16

Sometimes people laugh or mock, or even try to stop us from expressing ourselves. They may ridicule our faith or try to make us feel ashamed for believing in Jesus.

Romans 1 tells us we don't have to be ashamed of the gospel of Jesus because it brings salvation to those who believe! The Bible tells us in Matthew 10:33, "But whoever disowns Me before others, I will disown before My Father in heaven." If we are ashamed of Jesus and disown—or deny—Him in front of people in this world, Jesus will deny us to God. Remember what we talked about in the One Way devotion (page 54)? Jesus is the only way to God the Father and the only way to heaven.

When someone makes fun of you or makes you feel like you should be ashamed of Jesus, stand tall and be proud to call Jesus your Savior and friend. Show them the love of Jesus by being kind and telling them about Jesus. Then, pray for that person that they would come to know Jesus too.

LET'S REFLECT!

1. Have you ever been made fun of for being a Christian? Share how that made you feel.

2. Oftentimes when people make fun of someone, it is because they don't really understand. How can you help someone understand who Jesus is?

LET'S DO!

Today, we are going to make something special, a Salvation book! This color-coded book will help remind us of some of Jesus's most important principles. You can use colored paper or white paper and crayons. You will need purple, black, red, white, green, and yellow. On the purple paper, write "Purple is for God our King" and then write out the text of Deuteronomy 10:17. On the black paper, write "Black is for sin" and the text for Romans 3:10. On the red paper, write "Red is for the blood of Jesus" and the text for Romans 3:25. On the white paper, write "White is for forgiveness" and the text for Psalm 51:7. On the green paper, write "Green is for growing in God" and the text for 2 Peter 3:18. And on the yellow paper, write "Yellow is for heaven" and the text for 1 Thessalonians 4:17. Put the papers together like a book. You can give your book to a friend, neighbor, or anyone you want to share Jesus with.

Father, thank You that I do not have to be ashamed of You! Help me live proud of You and being a Christian. Help me share You with other people. Amen.

THE GOLDEN RULE

Do to others as you would have them do to you.

—LUKE 6:31

Have you ever heard of The Golden Rule? Many parents and teachers will often tell us this special rule because it is very important. It says, "Do unto others as you would have them do to you." But guess what? The Golden Rule is from the Bible! When someone tells you this rule, they are quoting Scripture from the Bible.

The Golden Rule tells us to treat others the way we want to be treated. Do you want someone to lie to you? Don't lie to them! Do you want someone to hit you? Don't hit them! Do you want someone to steal from you? Don't steal from them! Do you want someone to be kind to you? Then be kind to them.

We need to treat other people the way we want them to treat us. That is very important to remember. Read it again. We need to treat other people the way we *want* them to treat us. Even if they don't treat us good, we still need to treat them the way we want to be treated.

LET'S REFLECT!

1. Think of a time someone was unkind to you. How did it make you feel?

2. Think of a time you were unkind to someone. How do you think they felt?

LET'S DO!

Being kind to others is important. We need to treat them kindly, just as we want others to be kind to us. Today, we are going to have a Golden Rule Day. Before every action, stop and think, "Is this how I want to be treated?" If you answer "Yes," then go ahead! But, if you answer "No," stop and reevaluate your actions. Make sure you are doing this at home, school, work, anywhere you go. Remember, not everyone is going to be kind to you. Make sure you are not treating people the way they are treating you, but are treating them how you *want* them to treat you. Keep a list of all the Golden Rule moments and, at the end of the day, talk as a family about your experience with Golden Rule Day.

Father, thank You for the Golden Rule in Luke 6:31. Help me remember to treat others the way I want to be treated and to be kind to them. Amen.

TO TELL THE TRUTH

The Lord detests lying lips, but He delights in people who are trustworthy.

—PROVERBS 12:22

Lying is never okay. Sometimes we lie because we feel like we need to cover up something we did wrong, so that we won't get into trouble. "Who broke the lamp?" "It wasn't me!" Sometimes we lie so that we can get what we want. "I am starving, but I just need cookies." Sometimes we lie to spare someone's feelings, even though it hurts them in the long run.

There are many reasons why people think it's okay to lie, but the Bible tells us that the Lord hates lying. Lying to someone says two things. First, it says, "I don't respect or care about you enough to be honest with you." And second, it says, "I don't respect or care enough about myself to be honest."

Whenever we lie, we are hurting ourselves and the person we are lying to, and we are hurting God. We need to always be honest. Yes, sometimes we might get into trouble or hurt someone, but telling the truth is always better in the long run. Lying will make our punishment more severe and hurt people more. Telling the truth is always the right thing to do.

LET'S REFLECT!

1. Think about a time you lied to someone. Were they angry or hurt that you lied? Did it hurt you to lie to them?

2. Think about a time someone lied to you. How did you feel?

LET'S DO!

Lying often results in more lies. We have to keep lying to cover up the lies. Today, create two obstacle courses. Make one simple and easy to navigate. Make the other more difficult, with lots of obstacles to go through. After each person goes through both courses, sit down, and discuss which course was easier and which was more difficult. Everyone should agree which course was harder. Like that course, lying stacks more and more obstacles for us to overcome forcing us to keep lying. Discuss why being honest is important.

Father, thank You for teaching us to tell the truth. Help us always remember how important the truth is and help us to be honest. Amen.

LISTENING EARS

My dear brothers and sisters, take note of this: Everyone should be quick to listen, slow to speak and slow to become angry.

—JAMES 1:19

Listening is important. We should listen to those God gave to lead us, like our parents, teachers, pastors, and bosses. We should hear what they are telling us because it helps us to learn, grow, and become a better person. God gave us these people to train us and guide us. We should also listen to our doctors. What they tell us is important and can make a difference in our lives. God gave doctors the wisdom and training to help us be healthy and strong.

The Bible tells us to be quick to listen and slow to speak. This means that sometimes we need to close our mouths and open our ears. Listening to what people are saying helps us to get to know them better, it helps us to understand how they are feeling, and it can stop conflict.

Listening is a life tool that can save our lives or the lives of others. We need to make sure we are following the message in James and being quick to listen.

LET'S REFLECT!

1. Have you ever tried talking to someone, and they just wouldn't listen to you? How did that make you feel?

2. Is it hard to listen sometimes? Why do you think that is?

LET'S DO!

There is a difference in hearing what someone is saying and really listening to them. We can hear them but not really pay attention to what they are saying. We need to pause and really listen to them. Today, let's play a game that helps us to really listen to what is being said; let's play Simon Says! Give each person a chance to be Simon. If the Simon says, "Simon Says ___," then do that action. But if they tell you to do the action, but don't say "Simon Says," then don't! You must pay attention and listen for those two special words, "Simon Says." After each person has had a chance to be Simon, talk about the importance of listening to others.

Father, thank You for teaching us to listen. Help us to always use our ears to listen to You and those around us. Amen.

WATCH WHAT YOU SAY

A gossip betrays a confidence, but a trustworthy person keeps
a secret.

—PROVERBS 11:13

Secrets can be juicy! When someone tells us a secret, sometimes we cannot wait to tell someone. We feel like we are going to explode if we don't share! But we shouldn't always tell.

There are times people come to us and tell us something in confidence. Maybe they needed to get the words out, or needed our advice or prayer, so they tell us, but they don't want us to tell others. It can be hard to keep it to ourselves. Sometimes we hear other people talking about something or someone, and we want to tell what we heard, but we don't know if it was the truth.

When we tell news that wasn't ours to tell, or when we talk about someone behind their back, that is called "gossip." The Bible tells us that gossip betrays a confidence, but it also breaks God's heart. Gossip makes it hard for others to trust us, and it ruins relationships. We need to be people who are trustworthy. When someone tells us something, we need to keep it to ourselves. When we hear someone talking about another person, we need to walk away.

LET'S REFLECT!

1. Has anyone ever talked about you behind your back? How did you feel? Did it hurt your feelings or make you mad?

2. When you hear people gossiping about someone, what should you do?

LET'S DO!

Gossip has a way of growing. It starts off as one thing, and with each new person who shares the news, it grows. Today, we are going to demonstrate this through a game. Let's play Telephone! As a family, sit in a circle. Have one person think of a short, silly sentence. (Examples might be: "The sky is blue," "Elephants are gray," etc.) The player then whispers the sentence quietly into the next person's ear, saying it only one time. Then that player must whisper into the next person's ear, again only one time. This pattern continues until the last person receives the message. Have the last person say the sentence out loud. Did it change from the original? Probably so! That is how gossip is. *Parents, this is an important time to discuss with your children the difference between gossip and sharing information for someone's safety (such as when abuse is suspected).*

Father, thank You for teaching us how to stay away from gossip. Help us remember to stay away from gossip and keep a confidence. Amen.

YOU MATTER

But in fact God has placed the parts in the body, every one of them, just as He wanted them to be. If they were all one part, where would the body be? As it is, there are many parts, but one body.

—1 CORINTHIANS 12:18–20

Can you imagine if everyone was a schoolteacher? Then we wouldn't have doctors for when we are sick, mechanics for when our cars break down, or farmers to plant the food we eat! What about if our only sense was hearing? Then we wouldn't be able to see, taste, feel, or smell!

Every job is important. We need schoolteachers, but we also need doctors, mechanics, plumbers, cooks, maintenance workers, police officers, and so many other jobs. Our senses are all important. We need to be able to hear, but we also need to be able to see, taste, feel, and smell. Everything matters. Everyone needs to do their job to make the world work.

You matter too. If you are the parent, that is important. If you are the oldest child, that is important. If you are the baby, that is important. If you fall in the middle, that is important. Your place in your family is important! No one else can be you. No one else can take your place. Your family needs you to make your family complete.

LET'S REFLECT!

1. If someone came to you and said they felt like they didn't matter in their family, what would you tell them?

2. Do you ever feel like your place in your family doesn't matter? Share how you feel.

LET'S DO!

Sometimes our family needs encouragement to know they matter. Who better to encourage them than their own family! Today, we are going to do just that, encourage each other. Sit in a circle. Go around the circle, and when your turn comes, share one compliment about each person. Really dig deep and think about it. Share something nice about their character or their gifts and talents. Be kind, remember we are encouraging each other, not putting each other down. When it comes time for your family to encourage you, be sure to say "thank you"!

Father, thank You for reminding us that we all have an important place in our family, and we matter. Help us remember to show that to each other. Amen.

DON'T BE SCARED

He will not let your foot slip—He who watches over you will not slumber; indeed, He who watches over Israel will neither slumber nor sleep.

—PSALM 121:3-4

There are many things in this world that frighten people—spiders, snakes, heights, storms, tight spaces, and the dark, just to name a few. The truth is everyone is afraid of something. Satan likes to remind us of our fears when we are trying to go to sleep. He knows when we are lying there in the quiet, he can fill our hearts and minds with fear and keep us away.

The Bible tells us over and over that we do not have to be afraid. But why don't we have to be afraid? In Psalm 121 God tells us that He never sleeps. Never. He is always wide awake watching over us. If God, the Creator of the Universe, is always wide awake watching over us, we can trust that He will take care of us while we peacefully sleep.

When we feel afraid, we need to remind ourselves that God is there, and He will be protecting us. We just need to put our eyes on Him and trust in Him. We can sleep because God is awake.

LET'S REFLECT!

1. What is something that scares you? Why does it scare you?

2. How does knowing God never sleeps and is always with you bring peace?

LET'S DO!

Everyone is afraid of something, even adults. Today, we are going to give those fears to God so that we can sleep. Give each person a piece of paper and a marker. Toward the middle of the paper, have everyone write down or draw a picture of the fear that keeps them awake at night. Next, on the top of your paper, write the words to Psalm 121:3–4. Then, at the bottom of your paper, write "God, I give my fears to You. Amen." Place the paper next to your bedside, and before you to go sleep tonight, repeat Psalm 121:3–4 and your prayer out loud.

Father, thank You for always being there and awake to protect me. Help me remember that You are always there watching over me so that I can sleep. Amen.

OH, BE CAREFUL

Your eye is the lamp of your body. When your eyes are healthy your whole body also is full of light. But when they are unhealthy, your body also is full of darkness.

—LUKE 11:34

Think of everything your eyes see in a day. TV, books, people at school or work, neighbors, tablets, phones. Your eyes view so much throughout the day. Now, think of everything your ears hear in a day: TV, radios, phones, traffic, people talking. Your ears hear so much throughout the day.

There is so much influence in our lives every single day. We hear and see things all around us. It is never ending. But are we seeing and hearing things that are appropriate? Sadly, not everything on TV, in books, on the radio, and on our phones or tablets are appropriate.

What we see and hear takes root into our heart. Just like a plant, roots dig deep and begin to grow what was planted. If we let junk into our eyes and ears, it will take root and junk will be in our heart. But if we are careful to turn away from junk and only let the good take root, our hearts will be full of the good. Be careful what you see and be careful of what you hear.

LET'S REFLECT!

1. Think about a time you were watching TV or a movie and something came on that made you feel uncomfortable. Share how you felt.

2. When we see or hear things that are inappropriate, we need to walk away and tell a parent. Discuss as a family what you can do when this happens.

LET'S DO!

TV and movies can be so much fun! However, there are a lot of TV shows and movies that are not appropriate. They have things in them that do not honor God, and when they take root in our hearts, they grow junk. It is important to be careful about what we watch and listen to. Today, let's have a movie night with something that will make good roots! Pick a faith and family movie, make a picnic dinner or order a pizza, grab the sleeping bags, and have a family campout. Eat your dinner while you watch the movie, then afterward, pop some popcorn and discuss the movie until you fall asleep. (One great place to find faith and family movies is PureFlix.com.)

Father, thank You for helping us understand how important it is to be careful with what we see and hear. Help us grow roots of good things. Amen.

GO INTO ALL YOUR WORLD

Therefore go and make disciples of all nations, baptizing them in the name of the Father and of the Son and of the Holy Spirit, and teaching them to obey everything I have commanded you. And surely I am with you always, to the very end of the age.

—MATTHEW 28:19–20

The Bible is very clear when it comes to telling other people about Jesus. As a matter of fact, Jesus even commissioned us to tell other people about Him. Matthew 28 tells us Jesus's Great Commission—this is where Jesus told His disciples to go and tell other people about Him and to teach them to follow Jesus. Jesus's Great Commission is for us, too.

Jesus tells the disciples to go into all the nations. Now, that can be kind of hard for us. Not every person can go to every nation. God does call some people to be missionaries. This means they might live in another country and share Jesus. But not everyone is called to this. However, we can share Jesus with all the people in *our* world. The people in your world need to know Jesus.

The people God put in your world—your family, neighbors, friends, people at school, people at work, the people you meet—are the people you can share Jesus with. You can share Jesus by your words, but also by your actions and your love. And most importantly, you can pray for others.

LET'S REFLECT!

1. When was the last time you told someone about Jesus? How did they react?

2. Do you get nervous when sharing about Jesus? What makes you nervous?

LET'S DO!

Sometimes when we need to do something important, it helps to practice. Today, let's practice sharing Jesus. Take turns acting out what you would say to someone about Jesus. A few examples of what you can do include: share a Bible verse, tell them Jesus loves them, invite them to church, or ask to pray for them. After everyone has had a chance to practice, pray and ask God to help you share Jesus with others. Next, challenge each other to share Jesus with one person this week. At the end of the week, come together and talk about how the challenge went. Who did you share Jesus with, what did you say, and how did they react?

Father, thank You for the Great Commission. Help us remember that with You we have the strength to share Jesus. Help us become comfortable and excited to share Jesus with our world. Amen.

IT IS FOR GOD

So whether you eat or drink or whatever you do, do it all for
the glory of God.

—1 CORINTHIANS 10:3

Chores are not always fun. Who wants to do all that work when there is so much more we could be doing that is actually fun? Dishes, vacuuming, making beds, doing laundry, mowing the lawn, cleaning the litter box, feeding pets, taking the garbage out: so much to do, taking up time that we could be having fun!

Although all those things may not sound fun, they are important. If you don't feed the pets, who will? If you don't do laundry, what will you wear? It all must be done. The Bible tells us that no matter what we are doing, we should do it for the glory of the Lord. But how do we clean the toilet or mow the lawn for the glory of the Lord?

First, we must realize that we are blessed. Those dirty dishes are a blessing because God gave us food. The dirty laundry is a blessing because God gave us clothes. All those things are blessings from God, and we should thank Him. Second, we can use that time we are doing those dreaded chores and pray to God.

LET'S REFLECT!

1. What is a job or chore you have that you do not like? Do you have any that you like? What do you like about it?

2. What can you do to change your least-liked chores so that you are doing it for the glory of God?

LET'S DO!

A family is like a team. For the team to run smoothly and be successful, everyone has to do their part, even when it is not fun. Today, discuss chores. If everyone in your family already has chores, discuss what you can do to make your chore time go more smoothly and bring glory to God. Examples might include: playing worship music in the house to praise God as you work, or each person praying on their own, or even making a game out of it. Talk about age-appropriate chores for each person and how to bring glory to God through chores.

Father, thank You for giving us different ways to bring glory to You, even through something like chores. Help us do our chores and jobs in a way that brings glory to You. Amen.

OUR SUPERHERO

For the Son of Man came to seek and to save the lost.

—LUKE 10:19

Everyone loves a good superhero, right? Superheroes come at just the right time when the world is in chaos. They swoop in and save the good guy and punish the bad guy. They save the day and make everything right.

We have a superhero. Not a web slinging, cape flying, laser shooting, invisible superhero. Our superhero doesn't change clothes in a phone booth, drive a sporty car, or wear a mask. However, our superhero came to this world at just the right time and not only risked His life but gave His life up willingly for us. He was beaten and crucified, then came alive again, just to save us. He fights the enemy and always wins.

Jesus is our superhero. A hero who doesn't save us just because it is a good thing to do, He saves us because He deeply loves us and wants us to have a relationship with Him and live in heaven with Him one day. The Bible tells us that Jesus came to seek and save the lost. He came to save you. Jesus is the best superhero!

LET'S REFLECT!

1. Who is your favorite superhero and why?
2. Think about the ways your favorite heroes live up to Jesus's legacy through helping people.

LET'S DO!

Watching superheroes can be a lot of fun! But playing superheroes is even more fun! Today, we are going to play superheroes. There's a catch! Each person invents their own hero. Think of two superpowers you would want to have for your superhero. Next, come up with a fun name for your superhero. And finally, create a costume for your superhero. Once everyone is ready, have a fun day playing superheroes together. Be sure you take turns letting everyone be the hero to save the day!

Father, thank You for sending Jesus to this world to be our superhero! Help us remember that Jesus came to save us and cleanse us from our sins so that we can live with Him. Amen.

GROW LIKE JESUS

And Jesus grew in wisdom and stature, and in favor with God and man.

—LUKE 2:52

In the Bible we read about Jesus's birth, but then we don't read anything else about Jesus as a child until He was twelve years old. Joseph and Mary couldn't find Jesus, and when they did, He was in the temple sharing about God. The story says: "Jesus grew in wisdom and stature, and in favor with God and man."

Although we don't know much about Jesus as a young boy or as a teenager, we know that He grew wise and gained an important reputation. We also know that He pleased God and people liked Him.

We can grow like Jesus. No matter if you're five, fifteen, or fifty, you can grow in wisdom and stature, and you can find favor with God and man. To do so, we need to become wise in Him through prayer, Bible reading, and a life committed to God.

LET'S REFLECT!

1. What do you think Jesus was like as a child?
2. What can you do now to grow like Jesus?

LET'S DO!

Jesus grew in wisdom. How do you think we can grow in wisdom? As a family, discuss what this might mean. Jesus also found favor with God. Discuss how you might find favor with God. One thing we can do is to worship God. Worshipping God helps us to grow in Him and find favor with Him. When a family worships together, they grow closer to God and each other. Today, let's have some worship time. Using your favorite music outlet, play some worship music. Remove distractions like TV and phones. For approximately thirty minutes, play worship music as you sing along and worship God together. Don't be afraid to close your eyes, raise your hands, or bow down. This is between you and God.

Father, thank You for giving us what we need to grow in wisdom and stature and to find favor in God like Jesus did. Help us grow like Jesus. Amen.

PRAYER, OUR TOOL

Then you will call on Me and come and pray to me, and I will listen to you.

—JEREMIAH 29:12

Prayer is an important part of a Christian's life. It is one of our tools. A carpenter needs a hammer. A mechanic needs a wrench. A firefighter needs a firehose. A cook needs an oven. A hair stylist needs a comb. A princess needs a crown. Superman needs his cape. And a Christian needs prayer.

Prayer is our communication with God. Without the right tools, a worker cannot do their work. Without prayer, we don't have that line of communication with God. The Bible tells us when we call on God in prayer, He will listen.

When we pray, we can give thanks for what God has done, we can tell God how good He is and how much we love Him, and we can ask Him for our needs and the needs of others. But we also need to quietly listen to Him and let Him talk to us. Prayer is something we need to do on our own and as a family. Praying together makes us stronger as a family and stronger in God.

LET'S REFLECT!

1. Have you ever tried to do a job without the correct tools? Or play a game without all the pieces? Is it easy or difficult?

2. Do you pray daily? If not, why?

LET'S DO!

Prayer is important. Today, we are going to make a prayer bowl. Find a bowl; it can be any kind of bowl or basket. Then get a stack of sticky notes or a stack of paper and a pen. Place the prayer bowl somewhere that everyone can have quick access to it, like the kitchen table. Keep the papers and pen next to the bowl. Any time someone has a prayer request—for themselves or someone else—they can write their request on a paper and put it in the prayer bowl. Once a week, sit down as a family, and pull out the prayer requests and pray over them.

Father, thank You for listening when we come to You in prayer. Help us remember how important the tool of prayer is and how we can come to You regularly to pray. Amen.

JESUS FILLS US UP

The thief comes only to steal and kill and destroy; I have come that they may have life, and have it to the full.

—JOHN 10:10

Imagine you have a glass of milk. This milk is your happiness. You wake up in the morning, and you are full of happiness. Then your brother or sister picks a fight with you. Then your dog makes a mess you have to clean up. Then you can't find your homework or your car keys. Then someone at school or work is not being nice to you.

Every time something bad happens, it is like you take some water and dump a little into the glass of milk. The more water you dump into the milk, the more watered down it becomes. Pretty soon, the milk will be gone, and your glass will be just a glass of water. Pretty soon, you are having a bad day because of a few bad things.

The Bible tells us that the enemy, the devil, comes to steal, kill, and destroy. He doesn't want you to be happy. He will do everything he can to make sure you are not happy. But Jesus comes to give us life, He comes to fill us with happiness—just like if we take the jug and fill our glass back up with milk. With Jesus, we can have a full life even when the enemy comes to destroy our days.

LET'S REFLECT!

1. Think back on a time when you had a really bad day. What happened that made the day so bad?

2. What can you do to take your bad days and switch your eyes to Jesus?

LET'S DO!

Today, we talked about a glass of milk and filling it with water. Let's take that idea and play a fun relay game! This game is best played outside. If weather doesn't permit, lay blankets or towels down on the floor. Get two bowls of water, two empty bowls, and two sponges. At the same place on each of the empty bowls, place a fill-to mark with an erasable marker or a piece of tape. Place the two bowls of water at one end of the yard or room and the two empty bowls at the other end. Split into two equal teams, standing at the full bowls. Have the first person dip the sponge into the water, run to the other end, and squeeze the sponge into the empty bowl. The player should then race back and give the sponge to the next person. Continue until the empty bowl is full. The first team with a full bowl wins!

Father, thank You for coming to give us life! Help us remember that even when we have bad days, we can still find happiness and fullness in You. Amen.

JESUS'S HELPERS

"The King will reply, 'Truly I tell you, whatever you did for one of the least of these brothers and sisters of Mine, you did for Me.'"

—MATTHEW 25:40

Do you like helping people? Maybe you like helping sometimes, but other times, not so much. Helping others sometimes slows us down in what we want to do, or it takes away from what we want. Maybe a parent tells you to help a sibling, but you are playing and don't want to stop. Or for the parents, maybe a boss tells you to help a co-worker, but you know helping them will slow down your own work.

In the Bible, Jesus asked the people if they were helpers. He asked if they fed the hungry, gave water to the thirsty, gave clothing to the poor, and helped the sick. Helping is so important to Jesus that He even tells them, whatever they do to help, they are doing for Jesus Himself!

When we help other people, we are helping Jesus. Jesus likes when we take time to help those who need a hand. It could be helping your baby brother, helping your elderly neighbor, or feeding the poor, anything you do to help makes Jesus happy because you are doing it for Him.

LET'S REFLECT!

1. Think of the last person you helped. What did you do and how did it make you feel?

2. Think of the last time someone helped you. What did they do and how did it make you feel?

LET'S DO!

Helping others makes Jesus happy. Today, let's help each other! Write everyone's name on a slip of paper. Fold the paper and put it in a bowl. Have each person close their eyes and take a slip of paper from the bowl. Make sure it's not your own name! You get to help the person on your paper with one chore or activity. Maybe it will be helping your dad clean the garage, helping your mom cook dinner, helping your big sister clean her closet, or helping your brother wash his baseball uniform. Whatever it is, help with a happy heart and remember that you are helping Jesus.

Father, thank You for teaching us that when we help others, we are helping You. Help us remember to be helpful with a happy heart. Amen.

CAST AWAY!

Cast your cares on the Lord and He will sustain you; He will never let the righteous be shaken.

—PSALM 55:22

Everyone gets sad sometimes. Things can happen in this world that break our hearts. Maybe someone does something wrong to us, or maybe we lose someone or something we love. Maybe we are doing something that is hard for us, and sometimes we are sad for no explainable reason. Whatever it is, we all experience sadness.

The Bible tells us to cast our cares on the Lord. God loves us and doesn't want us to be sad and hurt. He cares about us and wants us to be happy, so He tells us to cast our cares on Him. He can handle whatever is going on, and He will take care of us so that we are not shaken.

Have you ever gone fishing? When you cast your line, you aren't just setting it down in the water—you are throwing it out as far as you can. That is what God wants us to do with our sadness and worries. He wants us to throw them out to Him as far as we can. We don't have to live with sadness. We can cast it to God and let Him take care of us.

LET'S REFLECT!

1. Think of a time you were sad. What happened to make you feel that way?

2. What did you do to cheer up? How does it make you feel to know that God cares for you when you are sad?

LET'S DO!

Have you ever skipped rocks? It can be so much fun! If you do it right, when you carefully toss a flat rock across the water (kind of like throwing a Frisbee), you'll watch it bounce farther and farther away. This is what we need to do with our sadness—we need to toss it to God and let it bounce farther and farther away from us. Today, pack a picnic lunch and visit a local lake, river, or pond. Practice skipping rocks, and ask an adult to help you learn the skill if it doesn't come easy. Once you've got the hang of it, watch as the rock jumps farther out. Pretend that is your sadness, jumping far away from you! When everyone has had a chance to skip rocks for a while, enjoy your picnic and talk about giving your sadness to God.

Father, thank You for taking our sadness away. Help us remember that any time we feel sad, we can cast our sadness to You, and You will give us joy. Amen.

YOU HAVE GIFTS BUT NOT EVERY GIFT

Each of you should use whatever gift you have received to serve others, as faithful stewards of God's grace in its various forms.

—1 PETER 4:10

Do you ever get frustrated when you can't do something? You're not alone! Everyone gets frustrated when they can't do things. There are two very important things to remember when it comes to things we cannot do.

The first thing to remember is that even when things are tough, we still need to try! Everyone faces something that is difficult. The key is to keep trying. You can ask for advice or for someone to show you how to do it, but don't give up. Keep trying!

The second thing to remember is that you might not be good at something, but you are good at other things! God has given each and every person special gifts. Let's say your friend is good at soccer, yet you struggle with it—but maybe you are good at basketball. Or maybe your friend is good at math and math is hard for you, but science is your subject. You aren't going to be a master at everything, but you will be really good at something!

Remember that God made you special and gave you great gifts. Use those gifts and be proud of them. When you come up against something hard to do, keep trying.

LET'S REFLECT!

1. Everyone share one thing that you are really good at.
2. Everyone share one thing that is hard for you to do.

LET'S DO!

God has given each person He created—everyone in the world—a special gift. He gave us these gifts to use for His glory and to help others. In our reflection questions, you each shared something that you are good at. Now, let's revisit those gifts and discuss how they can be used to help someone. Let your family share their ideas with you—they may be able to encourage you in your gift! Now, take your ideas of how to use your gifts and make a plan of something you can do in the next couple of days to help someone in your family.

Father, thank You for giving us each special and unique gifts. Help us remember that the gifts are from You so that we can bring glory to You and help others. Amen.

NOBODY'S PERFECT

For all have sinned and fall short of the glory of God.

—ROMANS 3:23

Take a slow look around the room. Each person you see has sinned. Your parents have sinned. Your siblings have sinned. You have sinned. No one who has ever taken a breath is perfect. The Bible tells us that everyone has sinned and fallen short of the glory of God.

When the world first began, God put Adam and Eve into the Garden of Eden. At this point, the world and all in it were perfect. Even Adam and Eve. They never sinned. But then Adam and Eve encountered the enemy, Satan, and he tempted them into disobeying God's command. Once Adam and Eve disobeyed, sin entered the world, and it was no longer perfect.

Now that we know nobody is perfect, and we have all fallen short of God's glory, how can we fix it? We need to ask Jesus into our hearts, and we need to work hard to live for Him. We still won't be perfect. We will mess up. In fact, we will mess up every day! The key is recognizing when we do wrong, asking Jesus to forgive us, and then trying really hard to not do it again.

LET'S REFLECT!

1. Think of something you did today that you know was wrong. If you feel comfortable, share it with your family.

2. Think of the most perfect person you know. Someone who is always doing good and is never in trouble. Guess what? They are not perfect after all. They sin, too. And although we can still look to those we trust for guidance, remember that we can all still improve.

LET'S DO!

We all sin. Every day we do, say, or think something that is sinful. Today, we are going to do a little experiment. Get a clear glass and fill it about halfway with water. Next, have each person add one drop of food coloring to the glass. Then, pick someone to carefully stir the contents. What happens? The clear water is no longer clear. That is what sin does to us. It makes us dirty. Now, very carefully, have an adult add one drop of bleach to the glass. Again, pick someone to carefully stir the liquid in the glass. How does it look now? Is it clear again? That is what God does for us. When we ask Him to forgive our sins, He washes us clean again!

Father, thank You for helping us to see that we all sin. Please forgive us for all our sins and wash us clean. Help us remember that when we mess up, we can always come to You. Amen.

BE TRUSTWORTHY

Whoever can be trusted with very little can also be trusted with much, and whoever is dishonest with very little will also be dishonest with much.

—LUKE 16:10

Have you ever been asked to do something and didn't do it—but said you did? Maybe you said you cleaned your room, put something away, or ran an errand, but it wasn't the truth. Maybe you forgot to do it, or maybe you did it but it wasn't done completely or wasn't done the correct way. Whatever the case, you didn't tell the whole truth, and that's called dishonesty.

When we are dishonest, we become untrustworthy. The Bible tells us that when we can be trusted with the little things, we become trustworthy with the bigger things. But when we are dishonest with the little things, we are untrustworthy.

It is important for us to be honest and trustworthy. Being trustworthy means we do what we say we will do, and we are honest. Families should be able to trust each other and count on each other. If you are asked to do something by a parent, you need to do it. If you didn't do it, just admit you messed up and then do it. Never lie.

LET'S REFLECT!

1. Why do you think it is important to be trustworthy?

2. When was the last time you were asked to do something and didn't do it even though you said you did? What was it, and why didn't you do it and say that you did?

LET'S DO!

Families should always be trustworthy and able to count on each other. Today, we are going to play a game. Gather paper plates or pieces of paper, two for each person, and crayons or markers. On one, you will draw a happy face. This is Mr. Trustworthy. On the other, you will draw a sad face. This is Mr. Untrustworthy. Now, run through some different scenarios. If it is a trustworthy action, everyone should hold up Mr. Trustworthy. If it is an untrustworthy action, everyone should hold up Mr. Untrustworthy. A couple examples of scenarios could be: your mom asked you to clean your room, but you just shoved everything under the bed, or your dad said you only had five minutes left before you needed to turn off a video game, but twenty minutes later you were still playing.

Father, thank You for being someone we can always trust. Help us be honest and trustworthy. Help us to always be able to depend on each other. Amen.

LOVE IS

Love is patient, love is kind. It does not envy, it does not boast, it is not proud. It does not dishonor others, it is not self-seeking, it is not easily angered, it keeps no record of wrongs. Love does not delight in evil but rejoices with the truth. It always protects, always trusts, always hopes, always perseveres.

—1 CORINTHIANS 13:4–7

There are two important truths we are going to look at today. First, the Bible tells us in 1 John 4:16 that "God is love." If we look at 1 Corinthians 13, we see what love is. So, if God is love, is God all those things? Yes, God is all those things!

The second thing we are going to look at is the definition of a Christian. To be a Christian means to be "Christ-like." That doesn't mean being perfect, but it means trying to live like Christ. So, if we put these two things together, that means we are supposed to be love. Now, reread 1 Corinthians 13:4–7 together, but this time, instead of saying "love," say your name.

How does it sound? Does it sound perfect or maybe you feel like it isn't true? We won't always be all these things. But as a Christian, we need work on being love all the time!

LET'S REFLECT!

1. 1 Corinthians 13:4–7 tells us what love is. When you read those verses, which one do you struggle with the most?

2. Which is the easiest for you?

LET'S DO!

Today, we are going to have a family day. On individual slips of paper, have each person write one thing that they would like to do together as a family. Examples might include: watching a favorite movie, eating a favorite dinner, or making a dessert. Fold the strips of paper and place them in a bowl. Have each person pick a slip of paper with their eyes closed. Once everyone has their paper, look at them together. The paper you picked is what you get to lead for family day! The key to today is remembering to act in love. Be patient, be kind, don't envy, don't boast, don't be proud, don't dishonor others, don't be self-seeking, don't get angry, keep no record of others' wrongs, rejoice in truth, protect, trust, hope, and preserve.

Father, thank You for being love and teaching us what love is. Help us work hard at being like You and being love. When we fall short, help us look to You. Amen.

SERVE ONLY GOD

You shall have no other gods before Me.

—EXODUS 20:3

Congratulations! You've made it through fifty devotions, fifty reflections, and fifty fun activities. But there's still more to go. Let's begin the final stretch with the Ten Commandments. God gave these commandments to the people of Israel, and He has given them to us today. The first four commandments have to do with our relationship with God Himself. The last six have to do with how we deal with others. We will dive into one commandment for each of the next ten days.

The first of the Ten Commandments tells us that "You should have no other gods before Me." God wants us to serve Him and Him alone. You may say to yourself, "That's easy! I am not worshipping or praying to anyone else." But let's look at it a little bit deeper.

What do you put before God? What is most important in your life? Anything we put before God, whether a thing or a person, has become our god. We shouldn't serve people, or even material things—like TVs, phones, sports, cars, toys. We should serve God alone.

If we truly follow the first commandment with all our heart, mind, and soul, commandments two through ten won't be hard—because we want to serve God and God alone, and we want to do what pleases Him and brings glory to Him.

LET'S REFLECT!

1. What is the most important thing in your life?

2. You probably never thought of that thing or person as your god, but if you put it before God Himself, it has become your god. What can you do to put God first?

LET'S DO!

Today, we are going to do an experiment that will help you see what it is like when we put God last, versus when we put God first. You will need to gather a clear jar or glass, dry rice, and small toys such as marbles or Legos. Have each person share two things they enjoy doing, such as watching TV and playing video games. As they share their favorite things to do, have them pour a little of the dried rice into the container. Once everyone has had a turn, add the small toys. Each toy represents something we can do to put God first, such as praying, reading our Bible, worshipping Him, going to church, etc. Was there enough room in the jar for all the things we can do to put God first? Now, empty the jar and start over, putting the small toys—things to put God first—in the jar first. Next, add the rice as you share two things you enjoy doing. Did everything fit? We need to put God first in all that we do so that we can have no other gods before Him!

Father, thank You for teaching us to put You first. Help us remember that You come before anything, and when we put You first, we will have no other gods. Amen.

NO IDOLS

You shall not make for yourself an image in the form of anything in heaven above or on the earth beneath or in the waters below.

—EXODUS 20:4

Today, we are looking at commandment number two of the Ten Commandments. Much like commandment one, the second is telling us to put God first. Basically, don't have any idols!

God is to be first in our life. If we truly put Him first, we won't have any idols that we worship. But sometimes we let things get into our heart and mind and they become idols. Now, you probably aren't making golden statues to bow down to like the Israelites did, but anything that comes before God becomes an idol.

Are we focusing on that sports trophy? Has it become so important to us that we think about it nonstop? Are we so focused on that TV show that we can't miss it, we watch it over and over, or we think about it all day long? Anything that we think about above God has become an idol.

LET'S REFLECT!

1. What do you wake up thinking about? What do you go to sleep thinking about?

2. When you think of an idol, what comes to mind?

LET'S DO!

The things we enjoy, like sports or TV, are not bad. We just have to be careful to put God before anything else and not make idols out of the things we care about. Today, as a family, discuss what you put before God and how you can change that. Make a schedule to be sure that God is always a part of your day. For example, do you enjoy watching TV as a family after dinner? How about scheduling a twenty-minute Bible reading session before clicking the TV on? Do you want to spend some time outdoors? Then plan a weekend camping trip or picnic, but make sure you are back for church on Sunday morning, or find a new church near your campsite to visit. Discuss this together and let everyone have a say.

Father, thank You for reminding us that we need to be careful not to make idols out of the things that we enjoy. Help us remember to always put You first. Amen.

HIS NAME IS HOLY

You shall not misuse the name of the Lord your God, for the Lord will not hold anyone guiltless who misuses His name.

—EXODUS 20:7

Today, we are on commandment number three of the Ten Commandments. This important commandment tells us that God's name is holy and is to be used only with respect and honor.

The words we say and how we say them matter. When we use God's name in a way that is disrespectful, out of anger, or even as a curse word, we are misusing His name and we hurt God. We must use God's name with respect and honor because God's name is special. This means we are careful to always give His name reverence.

The Bible tells us over and over that His name is holy, so when we speak the names of God—such as God, Jesus, Christ, Lord, Holy Spirit, or whatever name you use for God—it needs to be for worshipping His name or sharing His name. It should never be said out of anger. Never as a curse word. Never as a word of frustration.

LET'S REFLECT!

1. Have you ever used God's name in a way that doesn't bring respect and honor? Don't worry, we have all messed up with this. Just ask forgiveness and work hard to not do it again.

2. Think for a moment of how special His name is. No one else is named God. No one else can do what God can. His name is special; He is special.

LET'S DO!

Names are special because they represent who we are. God's name represents everything that He has done and continues to do for us. It is something we need to be careful to use in a way that respects and honors our heavenly Father. Today, let's play a game with names! You will need to gather four or five types of food or drinks in sets. Of each type, you want a name brand and an off brand. For example, you could use Oreos and a store brand of sandwich cookies. Have an adult place each set—the name brand and the store brand—onto a plate, with each brand's identity secretly marked. The adult can use a code word or special marking to know which is which. Then have everyone try to guess which is the name brand and which is the off brand. And, of course, take turns eating them as you go along!

Father, thank You for Your special name! Help us remember how important Your name is and help us to always use Your name with respect and honor to bring You glory. Amen.

A HOLY DAY

Remember the Sabbath day by keeping it holy.

—EXODUS 20:8

We are continuing with the Ten Commandments, and today we are looking at commandment number four. This commandment tells us the Sabbath day is a day of worship and rest. Most Christians honor the Sabbath day as Sunday.

On Sunday we go to church. This is important because we need to learn about God by hearing the message God gives to our pastor. We also require people in our church because we need a community of other Christians. We need people in our lives who will encourage us, lift us up, and pray for us—and people we can encourage, lift up, and pray for.

In addition to going to church, the Sabbath day is important because we need to rest. When we look at creation, God used six days to create the entire world and everything in it. On the seventh day, He rested. If God rested, we need to rest too. Rest doesn't mean to just sleep or watch TV all day. It means to reflect on the blessings and goodness of God. The Sabbath allows us to have a day of worship and fellowship with other Christians and a day to rest.

LET'S REFLECT!

1. How do you keep the Sabbath day holy? Do you spend time on the Sabbath reflecting on God's goodness?

2. Think of your church. What do you love about your church or Christian community?

LET'S DO!

The Sabbath day is a day that we set aside to go to church and to rest. When we spend the time reflecting on the goodness and blessings of God, we are keeping this important day holy. Today, create a Sabbath Day Box! You will need a small box with a removable top, such as a shoe box. Together, have fun decorating the box and write the words "Sabbath Day Box" on the top. Throughout the week, encourage everyone to write down on a slip of paper special things to do on the Sabbath after attending church services, and add them to the box as the week progresses. These activities might include: picking a special movie to watch as a family, making a yummy treat, writing down questions about the Bible you want to discuss, and other activities that will help you to rest and reflect as a family.

Father, thank You for the Sabbath day each week. Help us remember that You created this day and called us to observe it and keep it holy. Amen.

HONORING PARENTS PLEASES GOD

Honor your father and your mother, so that you may live long in the land the Lord your God is giving you.

—EXODUS 20:12

Commandment number five is the first of the final six that helps us in our relationship with other people. And today's commandment deals with a very important relationship—the relationship with our parents.

The Bible gives us a very clear message when it comes to our parents. We are told to honor our father and mother. So, what does it mean to honor our parents? Honor means to respect. To respect our parents, we need to obey them, speak kindly to them, speak kindly about them, and listen to them. As a Christian, we also need to pray for them.

Sometimes that's easier said than done! Parents tell us what to *do!* They tell us when to go to bed, what to eat, to do our chores, and to do our homework. They're always reminding us to do things like wash our hands or be nice. They don't always let us do what we want. How can we honor them when they are always telling us what to do!?

We need to work hard to listen and obey. When we mess up (and we will!), we need to be quick to apologize and make it right. We must remember that God gave us parents to raise us and help us. Parents aren't out to make our lives miserable; they are there to love and help us.

LET'S REFLECT!

1. God is clear that we need to honor our parents. Discuss what honor looks like. Give each person a chance to share.

2. The Bible doesn't tell us we outgrow this commandment. We are to always honor our parents. Now discuss what honor looks like as you grow older.

LET'S DO!

You are called by God to honor your parents. Your parents are called by God to honor their parents. Their parents were called by God to honor their parents. And the list goes on and on. Today, we are going to do a little digging into family history! Get a poster board or tape a few pieces of paper together to make one large piece. With a pencil, sketch a tree on your paper or board. Then, beginning at the bottom of the tree, add leaves, writing the name of a family member in each. Start with the youngest family member and keep going up through the generations. When you are done, talk about what honoring your parents looks like in everyday life.

Father, thank You for our parents. We know that you have given us parents to love and take care of us. Help us honor and obey our parents. Amen.

DO NOT MURDER

You shall not murder.

—EXODUS 20:13

We are continuing through the Ten Commandments, and today we are on commandment number six. This command simply says, "You shall not murder." Okay! That sounds easy enough, right? We aren't going out to murder anyone, so we are done. Right?

Wrong. The Bible tells us that murder is more than just ending someone's life. 1 John 3:15 tells us, "Anyone who hates a brother or sister is a murderer, and you know that no murderer has eternal life residing in him." Wow! If we hate someone, we are just as bad as a murderer.

Holding onto hatred in our heart is wrong. It puts a block between us and God. God created all people, and His people are special to Him. When we end someone's life or harbor hatred toward them, we break God's heart. If someone has done something wrong to us, we need to calmly go to them and make it right. It is important to forgive others when they have wronged us, and when we have wronged someone, we need to ask forgiveness.

LET'S REFLECT!

1. Murder is wrong. So is hatred. Think of someone you hate. Why do you feel this way? What can you do to fix this relationship?

2. Forgiving others is important. When we don't forgive them, the unforgiveness grows—just like a weed in a garden—and becomes hatred. Think of the people you need to forgive. Are you ready to forgive them? How can you go about doing so?

LET'S DO!

We know that murder, hatred, and hurting people is wrong. Think of a person you have felt hatred for, or maybe someone you hurt—even if by accident. It is important to apologize and make things right when we do wrong. Gather supplies to make cards. You can use construction paper, markers, crayons, stickers, and any other materials to create these cards. Have each person make a card for someone they have felt hatred for or hurt. After making the cards, gather in a circle and place your cards in the middle. Pray together for the recipients of your cards. Then deliver your cards.

Father, thank You for this commandment that teaches us to love other people by not harboring hatred in our heart. Help us forgive others and be kind to others. Amen.

BE FAITHFUL

You shall not commit adultery.

—EXODUS 20:14

We are two-thirds of the way through the Ten Commandments! Today, we are on commandment number seven. This commandment is important for people who are married, but it is also important for everyone to learn even before they get married.

Adultery means to be unfaithful to your spouse. In marriage, God calls us to be faithful to our spouse. To only have eyes for the one we married.

If you aren't married, the most important people in your life are probably your parents, grandparents, siblings, or maybe even your best friend. But one day if you get married, the most important person becomes your spouse. (And of course, God always comes first, before any of your important people.) You need to learn this lesson of faithfulness now so you can decide in your heart you will always be faithful.

You can begin to practice faithfulness now by being faithful to other important relationships and in other areas of life. We can be faithful by being trustworthy and honoring our word. If we say we are going to do it, we do it. We can also be faithful by being a good friend and by obeying our parents.

LET'S REFLECT!

1. Commandment number seven may be specifically for people who are married, but we can practice faithfulness even before being married. Discuss ways to be faithful now.

2. Think about some of the important things you might want in a future spouse.

LET'S DO!

Today's activity is going to be a little different, and it is going to require some big work for the adults. Often people who are married get so busy with life that they don't get a chance to go on dates or spend time alone together, especially if they have kids. Today, find another family with kids in a similar age range. Make a plan to swap babysitting so that each couple can go on a date! Invite their children over and make a fun night out of it while the parents go out, perhaps for pizza, popcorn, and movies. Then swap! On another night, have the other couple watch your children so you can have a date night.

Father, thank You for this important reminder that married couples should be faithful to each other. Help us practice faithfulness now in other areas of life. Amen.

DON'T TAKE WHAT ISN'T YOURS

You shall not steal.

—EXODUS 20:15

We are so close to the end of the Ten Commandments! Today, we are on commandment number eight. This commandment, like all the others, is very important. We don't ever want to take what isn't ours.

We know that taking something from the store that we didn't pay for is wrong. But let's think about at home. Is it stealing when we take something at home that doesn't belong to us? Yes, it is! Let's say your brother has a video game that you really want to play, but he isn't home to ask. If you just take it without checking, that is stealing. If your mom makes cookies and tells you that you can't have any until after dinner, but you sneak one before dinner, that is stealing. Any time we take something that we have not been given permission to take, we are stealing and going against God's Ten Commandments.

When we steal from others, we become untrustworthy. If we want to honor God and be trustworthy, we need to be careful to not take what isn't ours.

LET'S REFLECT!

1. Think of a time you have taken something you didn't have permission to take. How did you feel? How did the person you took from feel? Did you get into trouble?

2. How can you avoid stealing in the future? Can you make sure to always ask permission before taking what doesn't belong to you?

LET'S DO!

Today, we are going to play a fun game called "Doggie, Doggie, Where's Your Bone?" To play this game you will need a toy to represent the dog's bone. Have everyone sit in a row and choose one person to be the dog. The dog will stand on the opposite side of the room with their back facing everyone else, with the dog bone placed on the ground behind them. Quietly pick one person to sneak up and take the bone and hide it. Everyone will say, "Doggie, Doggie, where's your bone? Someone stole it from your home. Guess who." The dog will turn around and try to guess who stole their bone! Play this a few times, giving everyone a chance to be the dog. Once you are done, discuss the importance of not stealing.

Father, thank You for teaching us to not take what doesn't belong to us. Help us remember to never steal. Amen.

SPEAK TRUTH

You shall not give false testimony against your neighbor.

—EXODUS 20:16

We are nearing the end of the Ten Commandments, but let's keep going strong with today's commandment, number nine! What does it actually mean?

"False testimony" means to lie or make something up about someone else. We need to be honest. But we also need to be careful not to gossip or spread rumors. We've said it before—our words matter. We need to make sure that our words are honest and true. When we lie, we can't be trusted. People won't be able to count on what we say because we are not honest, and they will quit listening to us.

When we lie about other people, we not only hurt ourselves, but we are also hurting others. When we tell an untruth about someone, people begin to see that person in a different way. It hurts them and can cause them to lose friends. God doesn't want us to hurt people—He wants us to be kind to others. When we lie or give false testimony, we are not being kind.

LET'S REFLECT!

1. Has anyone ever said something about you that wasn't true? How did you feel?

2. Have you ever spoken something about someone else that wasn't true? Did you apologize?

LET'S DO!

Lying is never right; it hurts so many people. Today, we are going to play a game called "Two Truths and a Lie" that will help us determine the truth from lies. Have everyone sit in a circle and think of two truths about themselves—maybe a favorite color, a favorite food, or a hobby they like—and one lie about themselves, something that is not true. One at a time, go around the circle and have each person present their two truths and one lie, and have everyone guess which of the three things is the lie. Once everyone has had a turn, talk as a family about the importance of telling the truth and not lying about other people. Remind each other that lying hurts ourselves, other people, and God.

Father, thank You for being a God of truth. Help us remember that when we speak falsely about others, we hurt many people, including You. Amen.

DON'T BE JELLY

You shall not covet your neighbor's house. You shall not covet your neighbor's wife, or his male or female servant, his ox or donkey, or anything that belongs to your neighbor.

—EXODUS 20:17

We made it! We are at the final commandment of the Ten Commandments. Remember, these are the laws God gave to the Israelites and to us. They are important and help our relationship with God and with other people. Today's commandment tells us, "You shall not covet." What does "covet" mean?

To covet means to be jealous. When we covet something that someone has, we are jealous of what they have. God doesn't want us to be jealous of other people's blessings. He wants us to be happy and content with the blessings He has given us.

Sometimes it is hard because a friend may have something we really want! Maybe they have an outfit or a video game that you really want. Or maybe they go on a trip that you really want to go on. When we are busy being jealous of others, we forget the blessings God has given just for us. God blesses us every single day, and His blessings are special for us. We need to praise God for everything He does for us and everything He has given us. When we focus on praising Him for the blessings, we won't be jealous of other people's blessings.

LET'S REFLECT!

1. What is something you have been jealous of before? Why?

2. How can you focus on your blessings instead of other people's blessings?

LET'S DO!

One way not to be jealous or covet what others have is to give thanks for what we have. When we are busy praising God for His blessings, it is hard to grumble about what we don't have. Today, we are going to make a blessing jar. Find a clear glass or jar, make a label that says "Blessings," and tape it to the jar. Then prepare little strips of paper to fill in blessings. Each night at dinner or before bed, have everyone write down or draw a picture on one of the strips of paper of something they are thankful for, and then place them in the Blessings Jar. When someone starts feeling down about what they don't have or starts feeling jealous, pull the papers out and read how blessed they are.

Father, thank You for all Your blessings! You are good and have given us so much. Help us keep our eyes on Your blessings and not be jealous of what You have given others. Amen.

A STARRY NIGHT

Lift up your eyes and look to the heavens: Who created all these? He who brings out the starry host one by one and calls forth each of them by name. Because of His great power and mighty strength, not one of them is missing.

—ISAIAH 40:26

We learn from the beginning of the Bible, in Genesis 1, that God created the stars above. He placed them in the sky. Imagine if you had a handful of shiny silver glitter and you purposely set each sparkle of glitter, one by one, in the exact place you wanted them on a piece of paper. I wonder if that's what God did? Or maybe it was more like a handful of glitter tossed onto the paper?

Although we don't know exactly how God placed the stars in the sky, we know that He did. The Bible even tells us that not only did He place the stars but that He also calls each of them by name. God knows every star's name! How amazing is that?!

If God created each star on purpose and placed them in the sky on purpose, if He knows them by name and calls them forth, think of how much more important you are to God. He created you. He knows you. He loves you. You are even more special than the glittery stars above.

LET'S REFLECT!

1. Have you ever gone stargazing? Have you ever seen a shooting star? Share what you saw and how you felt.

2. Think of this: God created the stars and knows their names. Think of how much more He knows and loves you. How does that make you feel?

LET'S DO!

The stars are beautiful. It is so amazing how there are billions and billions of stars in the sky—and that God placed each one of them there and knows each of their names. That is incredible! Today, let's enjoy the stars God created. Grab your sleeping bags or blankets and pillows. And, of course, a yummy snack is a must! Head outside and place your sleeping bags or blankets in the grass. Tonight, relax under the stars and watch them shimmer and shine like glitter. If you are unable to lie down under the stars outside, you can use glow-in-the-dark star stickers or watch a video of a starry sky. If weather permits, you could even sleep under the stars! Discuss how amazing God is and how wonderful His creation is. Pray together and give thanks to God.

Father, thank You for the stars above. We know that You created them and know them by name. We know that You created everything in nature and called it good. Amen.

RECHARGE

Look to the Lord and His strength; seek His face always.

—1 CHRONICLES 16:11

Have you ever been playing on your tablet or phone, reading on your e-reader, or working on your laptop, and all of the sudden the screen goes black? Oh no! The battery died on you right in the middle of your favorite game, the good part of the story, or work that you were doing! That can be so frustrating. The only way to fix the situation is to plug your device in so it can recharge.

You need to recharge, too. There are many ways that you need a recharge. But today we are going to talk about the most important way: spending time with Jesus. Your phone or tablet works well when it is charged, but the battery doesn't last a year, a month, or even a week. You have to recharge it regularly. You need to recharge with Jesus regularly, too.

To recharge with Jesus, we need to spend time reading the Bible and praying, which is like plugging into the power source! This source will strengthen you so that you can go on.

LET'S REFLECT!

1. When was the last time your device battery died on you? Were you upset or frustrated?

2. How do you think we are recharged by spending time with Jesus?

LET'S DO!

Spending time with Jesus is a recharge for our spirit, just like plugging in our electronic devices. It is something important that we must do daily. Let's start a recharging challenge! Every time your devices—phone, tablet, laptop, gaming system—need to be recharged, instead of using the devices when they're connected to a cord, use that charging time to recharge yourself by reading the Bible. You can read alone or as a family. Just make sure you let your device battery charge all the way to 100 percent! This is also a great way to put away distractions as you read the Bible.

Father, thank You for reminding us that we need to plug into You as our power source. Help us remember to recharge with You every day. Amen.

THE ANTS GO MARCHING

Go to the ant, you sluggard; consider its ways and be wise!
It has no commander, no overseer or ruler, yet it stores its
provisions in summer and gathers its food at harvest.

—PROVERBS 6:6–8

Have you ever watched a colony of ants? These little bitty insects are hard workers! If you watch the ants, whether in the dirt or invading your picnic, they form lines and go to work to save food.

Ants don't chow down on their food right away. Instead, they gather their food and march back home to save it for winter. These ants know they must work hard and save. There are other jobs for the ants to do, too. Some ants build new areas of their colony, some protect the babies, and some protect the anthill. Whatever they do, all the ants have a job, and they all work hard.

We can learn from the ants. No, we don't necessarily have to save food for the winter months, but we do need to be hard workers. The ants teach us to work hard before we play. The ants don't play video games or watch TV and wait for the big boss ant to tell them to get their chores done. They know what must be done, and they do it. When you see something that needs to be done at home, do it. When you know your chores need to be done, do them. Be like the ant and march to work!

LET'S REFLECT!

1. What is your chore at home? Let everyone answer.

2. Have you ever watched a colony of ants working hard? What did you think?

LET'S DO!

Ants are hard workers, and the Bible tells us to consider the ways of the ant. We should be hard workers just like the ants. Today, we are going to be like the ants. As a family, discuss a project around the house that you have been wanting to do but have been putting off. Examples include: cleaning the garage, weeding the garden, washing the windows, or cleaning the closets. Let everyone share a project that needs to be done and vote on which one you will do. Then, as a family, tackle the project with the determination of an ant! You could also use today's activity to help someone else, such as an elderly relative or neighbor.

Father, thank You for the lesson about the ants. Help us be hard workers and do the things we know need to be done without complaint. Amen.

DON'T THROW OUT THE INSTRUCTIONS

Listen, my son, to your father's instruction and do not forsake your mother's teaching.

—PROVERBS 1:8

Baking is so much fun! Cakes, cookies, pies, brownies—the options are endless and delicious. But have you ever tried to bake something without the correct instructions? Picture this, you are baking cookies. You read the recipe and gather the ingredients. Then, you throw away the recipe because you already have all that you need.

You mix the butter, sugar, and brown sugar to the perfect consistency. You add the eggs and vanilla. Then you want to add the next ingredient, but you can't remember if it is a pinch of salt and three cups of flour, or a pinch of flour and three cups of salt. Oh no! You settle on a pinch of flour and three cups of salt. You finish the cookies, and then your tastebuds alert you that you were wrong.

Instruction matters. God tells us in the Bible to listen to instruction. The instruction of our parents is important, so is the instruction of our teachers and pastors and anyone in authority over us. Their instructions aren't to hurt us, they are to help us be safe and grow. Just like a recipe matters for baking, instructions from our parents and other authorities in our lives matter.

LET'S REFLECT!

1. What is something you were told to do by a parent or other person of authority that you didn't like? Why didn't you like it? If you really think about it, do you believe they were trying to keep you safe or help you?

2. When you bake, do you pay attention to the recipe? Why?

LET'S DO!

What is your favorite baked treat? As a family, vote on a treat that you can bake together. Once you decide on a treat, gather the recipe and supplies. Follow the instructions carefully, those of the recipe and your parents! Today, you are going to bless a family with your baked treats. Choose a family you want to bless. It can be a family at church, a family at school, or a family in the neighborhood. Package your treats and pray over the family. Then deliver your treats and tell the family they are in your prayers.

Father, thank You for the reminder to listen to instructions. Help us be a family who listens and obeys instruction from those in authority over us. Amen.

LOVE YOUR NEIGHBOR

"The most important one," answered Jesus, "is this: 'Hear, O Israel: the Lord our God, the Lord is one. Love the Lord your God with all your heart and with all your soul and with all your mind and with all your strength.' The second is this: 'Love your neighbor as yourself.' There is no commandment greater than these."

—MARK 12:29–31

We just read in Mark that we are called to love God. It even says this is the greatest commandment. But then it goes on to say the second commandment is just as important; it says that we are to love our neighbor as we do ourself.

Who is our neighbor? Is our neighbor the person who lives in the house or apartment directly next to ours? Yes! But it is more than that. Your neighbor is anyone around you at any time. If you are at school, your neighbors are your schoolmates. If you're at work, your neighbors are your co-workers. If you're at church, they are the people at church. If you're at the grocery store, your neighbors are the people at the store. Your neighbor is the person near you, and God tells you to love your neighbor.

Okay, so your neighbor is basically everyone around you—so how do we love them? We need to be kind to our neighbor, be respectful, be helpful, and show them the love of Jesus. This is loving our neighbor as ourself.

LET'S REFLECT!

1. Think back to a time someone was kind to you. How did they show you kindness? Do you think they were loving their neighbor?

2. Think of ways you can love your neighbors. Now, do it!

LET'S DO!

We are called to love our neighbors, just as much as we love ourselves. As a family, think of another family you can help, such as relatives, a family in your neighborhood, or a family at church. After you have settled on a family, discuss how you can help them. Maybe you decide to make and deliver a meal, help them with a project, or invite them over for dinner. Whatever you do, make sure that you are doing it with a joyful heart. And most important, be sure to pray over the family, asking God to help you show love to them and to bless them.

Father, thank You for teaching us to love our neighbors. Help us remember that our neighbors are anyone around us and help us to joyfully show love. Amen.

A PURE HEART

Create in me a pure heart, O God, and renew a steadfast spirit within me.

—PSALM 51:10

King David is known as a man after the heart of God. He loved God and lived for God with his whole heart. But even though David loved God and lived for Him, he still messed up. King David did something wrong. He coveted—like we talked about in the devotion, Don't Be Jelly (page 120). He then committed more sins trying to cover up what he did. But God knows everything. King David soon realized he had done wrong; he had sinned against God. King David asked God to forgive him. He asked God to create in him a pure heart.

God loves us. He knows that we will mess up and do things wrong. He knows that no one is perfect. He just wants us to come to Him. He wants to give us a clean and pure heart, and He wants to renew a steadfast spirit inside us. King David knew that if he cried out to God and asked for forgiveness, God would forgive him. When we mess us, we can ask God for forgiveness, too. We need to ask God to give us a pure heart that seeks to live for Him.

LET'S REFLECT!

1. Think of a time you did something wrong and kept sinning in an effort to cover it up. How did you feel?

2. How do you feel knowing that we can go to God when we mess up and He will forgive us?

LET'S DO!

Have you ever written on a dry erase board or chalkboard? You can write all over the board—writing lots of words, drawing lots of pictures, or just making a scribble mess! But with an eraser or cloth, you can wipe everything away for good. That is what God does with us. He washes us clean and gives us a new and pure heart. So let's play a picture guessing game! Get a dry erase board and dry erase markers, or a chalk board and some chalk, or a big drawing pad and some markers. On a sheet of paper, make a list of easy to draw things like animals, places, food, or objects like cars and trains. Cut the list up and place each slip of paper into a bowl. Divide into two teams. One person will then choose a slip of paper without showing anyone else. That person draws the object on the board, and their team guesses what they are drawing. Designate how long they will have for drawing and guessing, then move on to the next team. Keep playing until everyone has a turn to draw.

Father, thank You for forgiving us of our sins when we do wrong. Help us remember we can always come to You, and You will give us a pure and clean heart. Amen.

TAKING CARE OF GOD'S WORLD

The earth is the Lord's, and everything in it, the world, and all who live in it.

—PSALM 24:1

In our very first devotion together, we looked at Genesis 1:1, which tells us God created the heavens and the earth. As we continue in Genesis, we read how God created everything in the world, and all who live in it. Even Psalm tells us the earth and everything in it is God's. Everything belongs to Him.

We now know that God created this world, everything in it, and all the people. He is the Master Creator! But what does this mean for us? We get the honor and privilege of taking care of this gift God has given us with His world.

It is important to be careful to take care of the world and all that God created. We can do this in many ways, such as being careful not to litter, picking up trash, being mindful of the water and electricity we use, reducing waste, recycling, and taking care of plants. When we take care of the things in this world, we are taking care of what God has given us.

LET'S REFLECT!

1. What are your thoughts about the world being God's gift for you to take care of?

2. Have everyone share one way we can take care of God's world.

LET'S DO!

This big, beautiful world is God's gift, a gift we should always take care of. Today, let's do just that! Gather trash bags and gloves and pack a picnic. As a family, head to a local park or similar area. Walk around and pick up trash, be sure to stick together and work as a team. This is a great way to keep the earth clean. After cleaning up trash, enjoy a picnic together and discuss different ways you can take care of the earth as a family. Use some of the ideas from today's devotion and think of other ways.

Father, thank You for creating this world and everything in it. Help us remember how important it is to take care of the earth and how we can do our part every day. Amen.

DO I HAVE TO LOVE MY ENEMY?

But to you who are listening I say: Love your enemies, do good to those who hate you.

—LUKE 6:27

Wouldn't it be wonderful if everyone in the world were nice? If you got along with everyone all the time? If you could count on everyone as a friend? That would be amazing! Unfortunately, that is not the case. Not everyone is kind. We've all been teased, and we've all faced unkind people.

The Bible tells us to love our enemies and be good to those who hate us. That is a pretty bold statement. Wait, we need to love the people who make fun of us and the ones who bully us? We need to be good to those who are always making life hard for us? Yes! When we show love and kindness to those who are not always loving and kind toward us, we are showing them Jesus.

So what do you do if someone isn't being kind to you? The first step is to tell an adult. Talk with a parent or trusted adult about anyone who is treating you badly. The second step is to pray for the person who isn't being kind. Pray that God will give you the words to say and that He would help them with whatever is causing them to be unkind. God wants us to be kind to others, even those who are our enemies.

LET'S REFLECT!

1. Think of someone who has been unkind to you recently. What did they do that hurt you?

2. How did you respond to the person who hurt you? Were you unkind back? Did you pray for them?

LET'S DO!

Today, we are going to make a kindness board. Using a poster board and marker, divide the poster into eight sections. In each section, write a specific act of kindness. Include things like "Smile at someone," "Give a compliment," "Help someone," "Invite someone to play with you," "Talk to someone who is normally alone," and other kind acts. After you have completed that, lay the kindness board flat on the ground. Using a small bean bag or small stone, take turns tossing the bean bag or stone onto the kindness board. Whatever it lands on, that is the act of kindness you are called to do today.

Father, thank You for teaching us to be kind and loving, even to our enemies. Help us remember that You created all people, and we can show Your love to everyone. Amen.

GOD CARES

Cast all your anxiety on Him because He cares for you.

—1 PETER 5:7

God cares about you. You are important and precious to Him. He loves you, and He cares for you. He also cares for the things that you care about. If it matters to you, it matters to God.

Sometimes when people pray, they don't know if they should ask God for little things. They don't want to bother God for small needs, and think they need to save their prayers for the really big things. But God cares about everything we care about. If you are hurting, God cares. If you are upset, God cares. If you scrape your knee, God cares. If you are tired, God cares.

You can always go to God and pray. He loves when we talk to Him. Whether you are giving Him thanks for a chocolate chip cookie or your house, whether you are praising Him for a beautiful day or a nap, whether you are asking Him to heal your sick puppy or your sick grandparent, God hears you and cares. Talk to God. He'll listen, and He'll care.

LET'S REFLECT!

1. Think about a time that you were unsure of asking God for a need because you thought it was too small or too big. What did you decide to do instead?

2. How do you feel now that you know you can talk to God about everything?

LET'S DO!

Today, we are going to do things a little differently. Let everyone have a chance to share their favorite little thing to do. Maybe it is reading a storybook together, or swinging outside together, or dancing to your favorite music in the kitchen, or making homemade pizza, or wearing matching shirts, or watching a movie together. This week, work as a team to incorporate everyone's favorite thing into your schedules. Discuss how even those little things that matter to us, no matter how small they are, they matter to God because He cares for us.

Father, thank You for caring for us and what matters to us. Help us remember that we can always go to you, no matter how big or small our need is. Amen.

AS FOR ME AND MY HOUSE

But if serving the Lord seems undesirable to you, then choose for yourselves this day whom you will serve, whether the gods your ancestors served beyond the Euphrates, or the gods of the Amorites, in whose land you are living. But as for me and my household, we will serve the Lord.

—JOSHUA 24:15

God loves you so much. He created you to worship Him, and one day He wants to take you to heaven to live with Him forever. However, God gave *you* the choice. He wants you to make the decision to live for Him.

This is the most important decision you will ever make in your entire life, the decision to live for God. It is the most important decision a family will make, for their household to serve the Lord. But when you choose to serve the Lord, not only will you have love, joy, and peace, but you will be making the decision that will one day let you go to live in heaven with Jesus forever. How amazing is that?

If you are ready to commit to God, let's say a very special prayer together:

Dear God, thank You for loving me so much that You sent Jesus to this earth to die and rise again for me. I sin and I need You. Please forgive me of my sins and help me to live for You in all I do, say, and think. I love You, God. Amen.

LET'S REFLECT!

1. Did you say today's prayer? How do you feel knowing you are making this important decision to serve the Lord?

2. How do you feel about committing to being a household that serves the Lord together?

LET'S DO!

Now that you and your family have made the decision to serve the Lord, let's create a beautiful reminder to commemorate this day! Gather your supplies. You will need a poster board or wooden board, markers, and paints. Write in large letters: "As for me and my household, we will serve the Lord. Joshua 24:15." Next, let each person dip their hand in the paint and leave a handprint on the board. Then, have each person use a marker or paintbrush and write their name next to their handprint. And finally, put today's date on the board. Find a place in your home to hang your artwork. This is a visual reminder of your family's commitment to serve the Lord.

Father, thank You for this journey we took together. Thank You for helping our family make the decision to serve You. Help us to stay committed to growing in You. Amen.

GROW IN GOD'S LOVE TOGETHER

The Lord bless you and keep you; the Lord make His face shine on you and be gracious to you; the Lord turn His face toward you and give you peace.

—NUMBERS 6:26–28

Congratulations! You made it through seventy family devotions! I am so proud of you. I pray these months together have helped your family grow closer to one another and to God. I pray that you have a new rooted love for God and His Word, and that your roots will continue to grow deeper and deeper.

Just because you've come to the end of this book doesn't mean your family devotional time has to come to an end! I encourage you to keep up this precious time together. You can start again at the beginning of this devotional, you can find a new family devotional, or you can read straight from God's Word. No matter how you choose to go about it, make an effort to keep growing in God's love together.

I'd like to end this time together with a prayer. Would you join me?

Father, thank You for this precious family. Thank You for allowing them to pick up this devotional and join together to grow in Your love. I pray that you would touch this family and help them to continue to grow in their love for You and each other. In Jesus's name, amen.

INDEX

ACKNOWLEDGMENTS

I would like to thank my family for your endless love, encouragement, and support throughout this process. I am so blessed! I would also like to thank the Callisto team for this opportunity, especially to my editor, Brian Skulnik. Without your help this book would not be what it is.

ABOUT THE AUTHOR

 **Jenifer Metzger** is the founder and leader of Woman to Woman Ministries. She has a passion for ministering to and encouraging women. Jenifer and her husband Jeremy have been married nearly 25 years. Together they have four children, one son-in-love, one daughter-in-love, one future daughter-in-love, one precious grandson, and another grandbaby on the way. She calls her family her "blessings from heaven." Jenifer loves serving alongside her husband in ministry. She is learning to say yes to God and loves the journey He is taking her on. She blogs for Woman to Woman Ministries at W2WMinistries.org, as well as her own blog at jenifermetzger.org.